Trash

Trash

An Innocent Girl.

A Shocking Story of Squalor and Neglect.

BRITNEY FULLER

362.76092

1 3 5 7 9 10 8 6 4 2

Virgin Books, an imprint of Ebury Publishing
20 Vauxhall Bridge Road,
London SW1V 2SA

Virgin Books is part of the Penguin Random House group of
companies whose addresses can be found at:
global.penguinrandomhouse.com

First published in the United Kingdom in 2014 by Virgin Books

www.eburypublishing.co.uk

ISBN: 9780753555590

Printed and bound in the UK by CPI Group (UK) Ltd,
Croydon CR0 4YY
Designed and typeset by K. DESIGN, Winscombe, Somerset

Penguin Random House is committed to a sustainable future for
our business, our readers and our planet. This book is made from
Forest Stewardship Council® certified paper.

CONTENTS

PART 1

CHAPTER 1

We were going to be late. I was searching for my
right shoe and Mom was looking for a work shirt. It
was 5 a.m. and I was exhausted. Every morning was
like this – something was always missing.

'Britney, we've only got thirty minutes before I
have to be at work, and I still need to drop you off
at the babysitter's house. Get off your ass and find
your shoe,' yelled my mom, while tearing through
the laundry room downstairs.

I traipsed back upstairs and started looking
around. I'd found my left shoe by the couch in the
living room. The other one should be somewhere
nearby. Where was it?

You couldn't see the floor in my house. I had to
wade through piles of garbage, stacks of newspapers
and mountains of soda bottles to find anything.
I sifted through the trash, but I still couldn't find
my shoe.

I peered under the couch – *maybe it got kicked under there?* Nope, just some dishes, a doll I didn't play with anymore, some clothes and spider webs. I got up and kicked some of the garbage to the side of the couch to clear some space. Cool, there was the headband I lost a while ago. I picked it up and went to the bathroom to see how it looked on me.

I was too short to see myself in the mirror, so I climbed onto the edge of the tub. Wobbling, I grabbed the headband off the sink. Eww, some of the dried toothpaste on the sink was now stuck to the headband. I licked my thumb and tried wiping if off, but it was hopeless. The toothpaste had left a thick white smear.

'We've got twenty-five minutes. You better be ready when I find my shirt, or you're going to get spanked,' yelled Mom.

I nervously leapt down from the side of the bath. I didn't like spankings. I got one for every year old I was. That meant four spankings this time. Mom always liked to remind me on my birthday: 'Britney, you better be good this year. I can give you four spankings now.'

I scurried to the kitchen. Squeezing between the counter and the pile of trash in the doorway, I spotted part of a shoe under some food wrappers.

I plucked it out from the trash, but it was not the one I needed. I tossed it back onto the kitchen floor, and continued my search.

I lifted up the bag of trash we had started filling yesterday – *maybe my shoe is under there?* Yuk, a brown fluid that smelled like death dribbled out. *Thank goodness my shoe isn't under there.*

I headed to Mom's room. On the way, I popped my head around the door of my bedroom. No luck. There was just some paper, a few books and my bedroom furniture.

I went into Mom's room. That's where I slept too. I shared a bed with my mom because I was afraid to be alone with the rubbish. I was afraid of the scratching and the squeaking noises that would start in the middle of the night, and get closer and closer. At least I had my mom to protect me if I slept with her.

There was a lot more rubbish in Mom's room though. There was only a clear foot of space between the door and her bed; the rest of the room was covered in stinky rubbish and dirty dishes piled as high as my waist. The mattress had slid off its frame and was being held up by the trash underneath. I checked in the gap where the mattress should have been, but there were only a few soda bottles, some stained clothes and Blondie – my stuffed dog. I sat on the edge of the mattress and tried to remember what I did when I got home the previous night. I ate dinner, watched TV in the living room, played with Blondie, gathered dirty laundry …

That must be it! My shoe had to be in the dirty clothes pile. I jumped from the bed to the doorway and started ripping through the pile of clothes in front of the bathroom door.

I could hear the steps moaning under my mom's feet, as she clomped up the stairs.

'I found my shirt, are you ready to go?' she shouted.

'Yes,' I lied, desperately sifting through the dirty pile.

My heart pounded in my ears, and sweat dribbled down my brow. I didn't want to get spanked. I tossed the pair of trousers I had worn yesterday to the side and heard a hollow thud. *Maybe my shoe is caught in my trouser leg?*

The stair door swung open, smacking against the wall. Her big belly swung back and forth in her work trousers. She had a scowl on her face. Her eyebrows were furrowed, as usual, and her lips were pursed. She had a stone-cold look in her eyes.

'All right kiddo, head to the car, I just have to grab my purse.'

I found my shoe, lodged in the leg, just in time. I yanked it out and quickly put it on. My mom headed to the living room, where her purse was perched on the arm of the couch, while I made my way downstairs to the basement.

I waited on the stairs – our basement was scary, I didn't like being down there alone. Mom was at the top of the stairs, and started to make her way down. I waited for her and, when it was safe, I joined her walking through the laundry room to the garage.

All of our clothes were in piles on the floor as we didn't have wardrobes and drawers for them. In the winter, or on rainy days, our clothes got dirty – because we had to walk over the piles with muddy feet. The washing machine must have been leaking again because every step I took was squishy. I didn't like it when the washer leaked. My clothes stank, and the whole house smelt like a wet dog.

I had to be careful when getting in the car. I sat in the front seat since there was never room in the back. The seats were buried under McDonald's bags, soda bottles, clothes and a bunch of other mouldy containers.

I fought for some leg space. I stirred the soda bottles and trash with my feet until I was comfortable. Mom opened the garage door, and we headed off to the babysitter's house.

My mom looked at me with a smile on her face. 'Good job finding your shoe, kiddo. I'm not going to be late today.'

• • •

After school I was back at the babysitter's where I waited and waited for my mom to pick me up. I had something important to ask her. *She should be here any minute*, I thought, peeking over the windowsill.

'Britney, you should get your stuff ready and get your shoes on,' my babysitter shouted from the kitchen.

'Okay,' I said, skipping to the porch. I sat down, put my shoes on, looked out the screen door and there she was, pulling into the driveway. I bolted from the door back to the living room, and quickly shoved all of my stuff into my backpack.

'Britney, stop running in the house. Do you do this in your home?' scolded my babysitter.

I slowed down to a brisk walk and greeted my mom at the door.

'Mom, Mom. Michelle asked if I can sleep over, can I, can I?' I asked, pleading.

'Well, hi kiddo, nice to see you too. Maybe, I'll have to talk with Michelle's mom, and make sure it's okay. We'll talk about this when we get home,' she said grabbing my backpack.

'Bye, see ya tomorrow!' she yelled to the babysitter as she guided me to the car.

I was too excited to wait until we got home to talk about spending the night with my friend. I had never been invited to spend the night at a friend's house before. I didn't have many friends. The other kids thought I was weird.

'Mom, can I please go? This will be my first sleepover.'

'I know, that's why I said maybe. I have to make sure you'll be safe,' she hushed me.

'Well, if you don't think I'll be safe, then she can just spend the night at our house, right?'

My suggestion seemed to make her uncomfortable. She struggled to find her words.

'Um, it's not that easy. Her mom will also want to make sure she'll be safe and, well, our house is messy.'

We got home and I rushed upstairs to the living room. I sifted through the mountain of papers on the computer desk for the parent contact sheet. When I turned round, I found my mom in the doorway, making herself comfortable.

She took her shoes off, releasing the pungent odour that had been trapped all day. She usually didn't wear socks, and a black crusty dirt was visible between her toes. In one fell swoop, she slid off her trousers and underwear, and left them where they fell. She walked into the living room, taking off her shirt. She tossed it on a pile of rubbish bags and sat down on the faux leather couch.

Her stomach jiggled with every step. Her butt and thighs were riddled with zits. Some of them wept; others were red, with big heads, and ready to pop; and some were purple from her squeezing them too much. On her hip, just under her belly roll, was a cyst about the size of a ten-cent piece. It was always red and inflamed, from getting caught on her trousers or her underwear. Sometimes it would tear, causing her to bleed.

Her strawberry blonde hair was usually in a ponytail at work, but at home she wore it down and it just tickled her shoulders. But her dull green eyes always seemed to be scowling under her wild brows. Even when happy, she looked like she was frowning.

'That's her phone number. Call her, please?' I begged, pointing to the paper.

Mom sighed at my impatience. She rubbed her temples, closed her eyes and took a deep breath. After a few moments she held out her hand for the paper.

'Fine, go watch TV while I talk to Michelle's mom.'

Before going into our shared bedroom, I slid out of my clothes too. We never wore clothes unless we were leaving the house. I thought it was normal, because that's all I had known. I just copied my mom. Naked, I settled on the bed and flipped through the channels. I didn't care what was on, I just wanted to know if I could spend the night with my new friend.

After what seemed like forever, Mom came through and told me I could spend the night at Michelle's house. I was so excited. I had only spent the night away at my Aunt Maxine's house and grandparents' before.

'Thank you, thank you, thank you!' I bounced.

'No problem, kiddo, you'll ride the bus with Michelle after school on Friday. I'll drop off your sleepover bag after I finish work at the hospital. And, you'll behave. Okay?'

'Okay Mom,' I said, grinning from ear to ear.

• • •

The week went by so slowly, but finally it was Friday and I got to spend the night at Michelle's. I had my bus note ready, and we got on the bus together. They had assigned seats, but the bus driver gave us a break and let us sit next to each other. We were on the bus for what seemed like forever. She was the second to last stop.

Pointing to a big grey building, Michelle proudly said, 'That's where I live.'

'Oh, you live in an apartment? That's cool, I've never been in one.' My eyes were big as saucers.

The bus stopped and we were greeted by Michelle's mom. She took our bags and we walked up the stairs to her apartment.

She opened the door and I was speechless. They had a dining table with snacks and crafts laid across it. They had a huge pop-up fort in the living room, and everything just seemed to have its own place. Our dining table had junk piled so high on top, you could barely see it. Our chairs were buried under trash. You couldn't walk in our living room, let alone have a fort in the middle of it.

I headed for the fort but Michelle's mom stopped me.

'Sorry, but we don't allow shoes in the house. You'll have to take them off at the door and leave them on the shoe mat,' she said, pointing to a big rug next to the front door.

'I'm sorry,' I blushed.

'Come on Britney, my mom has a bunch of crafts we can do,' said Michelle, already sitting at the table.

There were boxes with markers, glitter, paint and crayons. All neatly packed together, and even labelled. They had rulers, and scissors, and glue sticks. The glue sticks weren't even dried out, they were so well looked after. They also had construction paper in every colour you could think of. My mom wouldn't let me have any craft supplies because it was impossible not to lose them in the rubbish, and anyway I didn't have a clear space where I could lay everything out.

Michelle and I did a couple of crafts, but I wanted to play in the fort.

'Come on Michelle, let's play video games in the fort,' I said, walking towards the den.

'Hold on girls, we have to clean up,' said Michelle's mom, sternly.

I was confused. Mom never cleared up anything.

'Can't we just do it later? It's not that messy,' I asked.

'We could, but why just let it sit there, and besides, it'll only take five minutes.'

It did only take us five minutes. It was super easy putting markers in the marker box, glitter in the glitter box, and so on. They also had a special place in the closet where all of the craft supplies went. In no time at all, everything was cleaned up and we were playing video games in the fort.

Nothing at our house had a place. Things just went wherever they were put or thrown. We didn't even put dishes away. They just sat around until we needed to use them.

I really like Michelle's house, I thought.

A while later, the doorbell rang. It was my mom.

'Hey kiddo, I've got your bag.'

'Do you see their house? It's amazing!' I beamed, beckoning her inside. 'You have to take your shoes off if you want to come in. See how clean it is? They even have a bin they can put their trash in. They don't have to bring it to their grandma's house.'

'Shh, don't talk about that. And I'm not staying, just dropping off your bag,' she backed off. Mom was acting weird. Why didn't she want me to tell Michelle's mom that we don't have any rubbish bins?

• • •

Michelle and I played video games, went swimming and played on the apartment's jungle gym. I slept in a clean bed with fresh sheets. It was so nice I fell straight to sleep.

Michelle's mom woke us in the morning, and let us help make the breakfast. We had pancakes, eggs and sausage. I had never had pancakes at home before, just at a restaurant or at Grandma's. I liked Grandma's cooking, I wished we could go to her house more than once a week. Mom didn't cook for us, she just brought home leftovers from her work. She was a cook, and had worked in bars, in a jail and now she cooked meals at a hospital.

Cleaning up was a breeze at Michelle's too. They had a dishwasher. I couldn't believe there was a machine you could put the dishes in and it did the rest. My mom didn't like doing dishes, and I wasn't tall enough to reach the sink. I had to stand on a chair to do the dishes.

Mom picked me up at noon. As we were pulling away, I pressed my face up against the window of the car, longing to go back to Michelle's. I didn't want to go home – Michelle's house was clean.

● ● ●

Back home, Mom dropped off the stuff she'd picked up at a garage sale and went to the kitchen to put away some groceries. It looked like she had got a few books, some clothes and an old vase. I scurried to the bathroom. Just as I was pulling down my pants, I heard Mom scream. I froze in fear.

After a few seconds of silence, I heard swatting and loud stomping noiscs.

'What's going on?' I yelled. I felt scared.

'Fucking mice,' she roared. Mom said rude words all the time.

I pulled up my trousers and bolted down the hallway, dodging the clothes and bottles. I rounded into the kitchen and nearly fell onto my butt as I screeched to a halt. There were two dead mice. Their furry bodies were squished and their intestines spewed across the dirty floor. Mom was swatting another mouse that she had cornered by the sink. It was too fast and got away.

I could see the anger burning in her eyes. I hated when Mom got like this.

She walked past me, grabbed my hand and dragged me downstairs.

'Where are we going?' I stammered.

'To the store to get mouse traps,' she barked, ordering me to jump in the car.

Mom made me wait in the car while she got the mouse killing supplies. I hated when she made me do that. The car smelt so badly I could barely breathe. Sometimes my lungs felt tight, struggling for clean air.

After what seemed like forever, Mom finally came out carrying a bag stuffed with supplies. She threw it at my legs and started the car. I peered inside to see a dozen mouse traps, rat poison and peanut butter.

I wasn't allowed to help set the traps when we arrived home. I watched with wide eyes as she took an old pizza box that was next to the oven, ripped it up into smaller pieces, and placed the traps on top of each of them.

Just as I was leaving the kitchen, one went off. There was a dead mouse in there already!

We caught three more before bed.

As I lay in bed next to Mom, I couldn't sleep. Every time I closed my eyes, I imagined the mouse guts on the kitchen floor. I listened to the familiar scratching noises get closer and closer to our bed.

Maybe the noises were being made by the mice?

I strained my ear some more and I could hear them scurrying through the garbage, nibbling on the newspaper. Every once in a while, one would squeak. As I was drifting off to sleep, the snap of a trap sliced through the silence, followed immediately by an awful squeal of pain. As I was about to get up, Mom grabbed my shoulder and shook her head.

'It'll be over soon, go to sleep,' she hushed.

But I couldn't go to sleep. I looked at the rubbish swamping our bed and I felt funny. All of the junk seemed to close in on me.

I didn't like my house anymore.

CHAPTER 2

'Hey Britney, your uncle and aunt are going to be out tonight and they can't find a place for your cousin Louise to stay. She's going to spend the night with us.'

'Really? Can we rent movies and get pizza?' I asked. I was so excited.

'Sure, we're going to pick her up. We'll get that stuff on the way back.'

Even though I was eight now, Louise was the first person to ever spend the night at my house. Up until that moment, any time I asked my mom if someone could come over, she would either change the subject or suggest I go to their house.

I'd stayed over at a few friends' houses and I'd always had fun. I wanted to make sure Louise had a good time too. In the car, on the way to Louise's house, I started to get nervous. All the homes I'd been to were clean, and they had video games, playgrounds nearby and lots of toys to play with. My house was a mess, I wasn't allowed to have video games and we lived off a freeway.

Our house was huge, especially for just the two of us. Above the garage and laundry room we had three bedrooms, a big living room and a giant kitchen, all on one floor. But all that space meant there was more trash. The third bedroom was full of old broken furniture and cat poop. I couldn't run through the living room; instead we had paths which weaved in between the rubbish. We could only use some of the kitchen because the rest of it was buried under trash. Mom never wanted to throw anything away. She had piles of newspapers that dated back years. Mom would get really angry with me if I tried to move them.

We pulled up to my Aunt Maxine's house and went inside. Louise, her daughter, was sitting on the floor in front of the TV, playing with Lego. I was jealous of her. Louise was pretty, she was half Asian, and always looked like she had a perfect tan. Her hair was dark brown and straight, ending just above her butt. Even though she was the youngest out of four, her clothes were always nice. They weren't stained and didn't have holes in them, like mine. I was only a few months older than Louise, but we looked completely different.

I was very pale and never tanned, just burned. My rarely brushed hair had never been past my shoulders. She had lost her baby fat, and was slender and tall. I was short and chubby, and I always seemed to be oozing out of my clothes.

'Hi Louise,' I said excitedly. 'We're going to get pizza and rent movies. Is there anything else you want to do?'

'Um, I don't know. We can play games too, maybe?' she asked.

'Well, not really.' I hesitated. 'I don't have board games, and I've only got a few Barbies.'

'That's okay, I don't really like Barbie anyway. We can just watch movies.'

'Well, we have the internet too. We can play computer games,' I boasted, hoping she wouldn't mind the education games Mom did let me play.

On our way out, Aunt Maxine pulled Louise to the side. Even though she was whispering, I could hear what she said.

'Louise, you need to be polite and not say anything about the mess. Okay? It's just for tonight, I promise you won't have to go over there ever again,' she hushed.

My heart sank. She didn't want to come over to my house. *I'll ask Mom to get snacks*, I thought,

and only the kind of pizza and movies Louise wants.
Hopefully by the end of her stay, she won't even
notice the mess and she'll want to come back over.

I had to let anyone who drove with us sit in the
front. My mom told me it was polite, but the real
reason of course was because you can't fit in the
back seat for all the trash. I opened the back door
and a bunch of garbage fell out. I picked it up, and
tossed it to the far side of the seat. I grabbed more
handfuls of trash and tossed it across, until I finally
made enough space for me to sit down. There
was no leg room whatsoever, so I had to sit cross-
legged. My legs always fell asleep when I sat in the
back seat. Things poked at me, and it was very
uncomfortable. I also couldn't buckle up, because
trash was covering the lock.

Louise hopped in the front seat. She started
kicking around the trash at her feet.

'Why don't you guys just throw this stuff away?'
she grimaced.

'I don't really know,' I replied. Mom didn't
answer.

Why doesn't Mom want to throw the rubbish
away? I didn't understand.

We pulled up to the movie store. Louise picked
out a couple of scary movies and some cartoons for

us to watch. I liked her choices. The pizza place was next door, and we headed over and started looking at the menu.

'What kind of pizza do you like Louise?' I asked.

'Sausage, I don't like anything else.'

'Sausage is yummy. I just don't like the vegetables, they get gross when cooked,' I said, wrinkling my nose.

Turning to Mom, I announced, 'Can we get a sausage pizza? Louise doesn't like any other toppings, and I don't like the veggies.'

Mom rolled her eyes. 'No, we're going to get a supreme. That's what I like. You two can pick off the other toppings. I didn't ask for her to be here tonight.'

Louise turned to me with big eyes. 'But Britney, I don't like all of those toppings, I only like sausage.'

Embarrassed by my mom, I stared at the floor and said, 'She says you can just pick off the toppings you don't like. She won't get anything else.'

'Fine. I just won't eat,' Louise said curtly.

We jumped in the car and I put the pizza on my lap. It was warm and felt good on my legs.

'Mom, can we stop by a gas station and get soda and snacks?' I asked, trying to make up for the pizza.

'I guess. You each can pick out a two litre, a bag of chips and a chocolate bar.'

When we finally pulled into our garage, I carried the pizza, Louise took the snacks and Mom grabbed Louise's bag. In order to get upstairs we had to go through the laundry room, and walk across the damp clothes that were scattered on the floor.

Louise didn't know what to do.

'How do I get upstairs? Do I just walk on the clothes? How do I know if they're clean?' she squeaked.

'Don't worry about it, just come on,' Mom dismissed her.

Louise stepped carefully, trying to find floor to walk on, instead of our clothes. She moved too slowly, and was blocking my path to upstairs.

'It's really okay, just go,' I said, from behind.

She picked up her pace, and we made our way upstairs. She opened the basement door, and froze. She stared at the living room in front of her, and then at the kitchen, to the left. I knew she was looking at the piles of rubbish, everywhere.

Oh my God, no.

She was looking at my mom. Mom wasn't wearing trousers anymore. I thought she would keep her clothes on when someone was over to stay.

Mom flopped onto the couch, causing the clothes next to her to avalanche onto the floor. Before flipping through the channels, she took her shirt off and she slouched in just her bra and panties. She stared at the pizza box in my hands. Impatiently, she cleared her throat, waiting for me to bring it to her.

'Um, Louise, you can sit here,' I said, tossing the newspapers off the computer chair.

I put the pizza on the arm of the couch and offered Louise a slice. Louise's eyes kept darting, nervously, between the TV and my half-naked mom. I could tell she was looking at my mom's belly, which had pizza grease and sauce running down it. Louise looked disgusted.

'Like I said at the pizza place, I just won't eat it,' she said, crossing her arms. She shifted in the chair nervously.

I tried to make her feel more at home by pretending nothing was wrong. I wanted Louise to be happy.

'Mom, can we watch the movies we rented?'

I looked across to Louise, hoping that would cheer her up. Louise was too busy staring at a pile of mouldy takeaway containers. She looked like she wanted to run away.

'No, I'm watching TV. When I go to bed, you guys can watch them.'

'But why can't you watch TV in your room? You have a TV in there?' I pressed, desperate to make Louise feel more comfortable.

'Jesus Christ,' she yelled, getting up from the couch. 'Do whatever the fuck you want.'

Mom went to her room, and wrestled the door shut. *She's never shut her door before. What's that about?*

Louise looked petrified. I don't think my aunt used swear words.

My head was spinning – both Mom and Louise were now upset. I wanted to make things better, but I didn't know how.

'So, what do you want to watch first?' I asked.

'I don't care, I just want to go home.' Louise looked like she was about to cry.

Don't cry, please don't cry.

I grabbed the first movie I touched, and put it in the DVD player. We both watched in silence, not enjoying it, but counting the seconds that passed by. The movie ended, and I put in another.

Louise was frozen to the chair like a statue. She hugged her knees into her chest and there was a dewy sheen under her eyes. She had been crying.

'Britney, I'm really hungry. Do you have anything else to eat?' Louise sniffled.

'We have vegetable soup I can microwave for you.'

Louise nodded and I hopped off the couch. In the kitchen we didn't have any clean dishes. There was a mountain of plates piled to the side of the sink. Flies were feeding off the hard crusty remains. I spotted a fresh mouse kill beside the fridge. I blanked it out and just got on with washing up a coffee cup. I heated up the soup and grabbed a plastic spoon. I peeked around the kitchen door to see if Louise had stopped crying and I caught her wiping her eyes.

'Here you go,' I smiled, handing her the soup that looked a lot like swamp water.

Louise looked at it strangely, but started eating.

After she was finished, she turned to me, gesturing to the dirty cup and spoon. 'Where should I put this?'

'Oh, just put it on the floor.'

She looked at me like I was weird.

The time ticked by. It was 11.30, hours later than my normal bedtime. 'I'm bored,' Louise said. 'Is there anything to do?'

Thinking for a second, I said, 'Actually, I like making my own shampoo.'

'Really?' She looked at me like I was a total freak. Everything I was doing was upsetting her, and

I didn't know why. I was feeling more and more desperate.

'Yeah, I take the shampoo we have and mix it with conditioners. I make my own scents from the ones we already have. And we have plenty of old bottles. We have everything in the bathroom,' I said, leading her down the hall towards the bathroom.

I picked up two empty shampoo bottles from next to the toilet, and wiped off the cobwebs. I handed one to Louise, grabbed all of the half full shampoo bottles, and put them in the bath.

'I just mix the ones that smell the best,' I said, squeezing shampoo into my bottle.

Rolling her eyes, Louise said, 'This is stupid, I'm going to play on the computer.'

She took a few steps down the hall. Then there was silence.

Why has she stopped? For a moment, all I could hear was my mom's snoring vibrating down the hall.

Oh God, she's stopped outside Mom's room.

'Why doesn't your mom have a doorknob?' she asked, fingering the hole where the handle should be.

My heart dropped. The shampoo bottles I was holding fell to the ground as I lunged towards Louise. But it was too late. She had peered through the hole into Mom's room.

Louise gasped. She stumbled back, tumbling over a pile of dirty clothes. She staggered to her feet with a look of horror on her face, her eyes as big as saucers.

'Oh. My. God. Britney. Your mom is sleeping naked. She looks like a beached whale. Why did you let me look in there?'

I was so embarrassed. I snapped back at her like a cornered dog.

'I didn't know what you were doing. You shouldn't be looking in other people's rooms anyway.'

I headed back to the living room and tossed a blanket to Louise.

'You can sleep on the couch, I'll sleep on the beanbag,' I barked.

I just wanted this night to be over with.

I disappeared to Mom's room and quietly crept into bed beside her. As I lay awake listening to her snoring, my mind raced with thoughts I couldn't understand. I was angry with Mom for destroying my first sleepover. But I was also angry at Louise for being so mean about my mom. What I was becoming certain about though, was that something was very wrong about the way we lived.

You could have cut the atmosphere with a knife the next morning. Louise couldn't bring herself to look at me and I didn't want to speak to her. I was afraid that she was going to say more horrible things and I didn't want to feel upset again. I was relieved when she left to go home.

I didn't want anyone else spending the night ever again.

CHAPTER 3

After the disastrous weekend with Louise, I was glad to go back to school. But by the end of the day, I was in tears.

'What's wrong kiddo?' Mom asked when she saw me crying at the school gates.

I could barely speak, I was so upset.

'It was show and tell today. Everyone had something from their dad. Where's my daddy?'

As soon as the word 'daddy' left my mouth, I began to sob, burying my face in my mom's shoulder. Without saying a word, Mom bundled me into the car, grabbed my rucksack, and we headed home. There was a deathly silence in the car, the radio was off, the only thing you could hear was my sniffles.

When we got home, Mom guided me upstairs and through the sea of trash in our bedroom. Snuggling up in bed, she wiped my tears away.

'Kiddo, your dad doesn't know anything about you. I don't even know if he remembers me. A little while before you were born, I went on a cruise to Europe. I met a very nice man. I don't even remember his name. I think it started with an A, maybe an E, I don't know.' She trailed off.

'But it's not fair. Why does everyone else get a dad? Can you find him?' I sniffled.

Massaging her temples, she snapped, 'It's not like I planned you. I didn't *try* to leave you fatherless. He got off in Europe, and I continued back here to the States. Like I said, I don't even know his name, I had had a few drinks.'

Her words stung. *She didn't want me, I was an accident.*

I scrambled out of bed and frog jumped over the pile of shoes and clothes to the living room. I crouched down in a clearing on the floor and cried my eyes out.

• • •

The next day I ended up hating myself even more.

The bell rang, letting us know it was time for recess. Everyone sprang up from their desks running for the door. I was amongst the stampede of kids, when my teacher called my name.

'Britney, I need to speak with you.'

'Yes, Mr Portsly?' I asked nervously.

The last of my classmates shuffled out of the room, looking over their shoulders, intrigued as to why I was called back. Looking at the floor, I could feel their stares. My teacher waited for the door to close.

'Um, I'm not really sure how to say this, so here it goes. Britney, and a couple of the other teachers think you smell. We want to help you out.'

Too embarrassed to respond, I just stood there, staring at him. My cheeks burned with embarrassment and tears welled in my eyes. *What does he mean, I smell?* I resisted the urge to smell my armpits and clothes.

Putting a hand on my shoulder to comfort me, he said, 'Kids your age go through a lot of changes. Your body starts making changes. Do you have a washing machine at home? Have you started using deodorant?'

I couldn't look at him anymore. I stared at the floor.

'I do the laundry, and my mom says I don't need deodorant yet, I'm only eight,' I replied sheepishly.

'Okay, well when I was younger, I would sometimes leave a load in the washer for a day or so and it would get sour. Do you sometimes wait to change it to the dryer? If so, that might be what smells,' he said kindly.

Still staring at the floor, I shook my head.

'I finish all of the laundry the day I do it.'

He patted my back, 'Hmm, well just remember not to leave laundry in the washer, and maybe ask your mom to help you find a deodorant. Now go ahead and play.'

He opened the door to let me outside. I could see the pain on his face – he hadn't wanted to have that conversation just as much as I hadn't wanted to hear it.

That burning ball of desperation was beginning to rise in my stomach again, as I shuffled outside with my arms glued tightly to my sides. I waited for the door to shut. When I heard the door click, I lifted my arms and sniffed at my armpits. I didn't smell anything, but someone obviously did. I lifted my shirt to my nose and took a big whiff. Again, I didn't smell anything out of the ordinary. Whatever I smelt of, I didn't even notice it anymore.

The bell was going to ring in a few minutes, and I didn't feel like playing with other kids. If the teachers said I smell, then the kids in my class would surely smell me too.

I headed to the bathroom instead. I had to wash the smell off me. *I must be disgusting.* I locked the cubicle door and slumped onto the toilet seat. I pulled at my hair in frustration and helplessness. I must have pulled hard, because when I saw my hands, there were clumps of brown hair tangled between my fingers.

It's so unfair. Mr Portsly and the other teachers think I smell and it's my fault. It's not my fault. We live in a pile of garbage. I'm not doing laundry the wrong way, the smell of the house is on my clothes and on my skin.

My eyes prickled from the tears I could feel building. I looked at my stinky shirt – it was threadbare and didn't match the rest of my clothes.

I tugged at my hair again in anger. *I'm such a mess.*

I burst into tears and cradled my head into my hands. I wanted to disappear.

I couldn't just run away though. I had to somehow survive the rest of the day. So, through the tears, I took my shirt off and drained the soap dispenser. The soap didn't smell too good, but it surely smelt better than I did. I worked up a lather between my palms and started with my arms. I pressed the soapsuds so hard, it was like I was trying to clean under my skin. I rubbed in small circles across my stomach and then worked my way up to my stinky armpits. I was scrubbing my body so hard, I started turning red and leaving scratches. I didn't care, I was going to smell good.

Scrubbing myself made me feel a bit better, but it didn't release the tension inside me. I wanted to scream. I wanted to yell my head off. Let the anger out because it wasn't my fault. But I couldn't; it would have got someone's attention. That was the last thing I wanted – people noticing me.

I rinsed off, the best I could, trying to go quick so I wouldn't be late for the next class. I was about to put my shirt back on when I noticed the automatic air freshener on the wall. I doused my shirt in 'Fresh Rain', desperately hoping that it would mask the smell of me and my home. I took the air freshener to hide in my desk, so I could spray myself down throughout the day.

I looked at myself in the mirror. I had the same scruffy brown hair over the same chubby face, only my eyes were puffy from crying. I'd hoped I was going to look cleaner, but that hadn't happened.

Tears started welling up again, *I just want to fit in. I don't want to be the weird girl in the nasty house who always smells.*

• • •

I heard the muffled sound of the bell ringing. I had two minutes to line up at the door. I quickly mopped up the mess I'd made and went back to class.

Mr Portsly welcomed me back, but I couldn't make eye contact with him. We studied math, which was my favourite subject, but after being told I smelt, I just wanted to hide. I felt like a turtle – I wanted to be able to shrink back into my shell and block out the world. I wanted to disappear.

I didn't participate in class all day. I was afraid that if I raised my hand, the people around me would smell my armpits. Instead I sat low in my seat, hoping not to be noticed by anyone.

I found myself constantly watching the reactions of my classmates. I must have done a good job of washing myself and using the air freshener, because nobody scrunched their noses when I got close to them. I realised I knew what to look for. We were having story telling in the library last week and some of the girls had wrinkled their noses in disgust. We were all crammed together like sardines. I had tried to help everyone near me figure out who it was that smelt so badly, but now I knew it was me.

I didn't go outside for the rest of the break times. I didn't want to work up a sweat and make myself smell even more than I already did. I ate my lunch, alone, in the library. Later, on the bus, I made sure that I put my backpack on the seat next to me. Nobody was going to be able to sit with me and have a chance to smell me. I sunk low in the seat, and lost myself in the music on my CD player.

I was so relieved to see my stop approach. *I'll do my homework at the babysitter's house, then I'll wash all of my clothes when I get home. I will make this right, I will.*

• • •

Mom picked me up a few hours later. She sensed I was sad.

'Kiddo, what's wrong?' she asked, as she drove us home.

I wasn't sure how to respond; she wasn't going to care that the teachers thought I smelt. She didn't care how the house or car looked or smelt, so why would she care if I smelt?

'Oh, nothing. I just have a headache,' I lied.

'Come on now, I know you. What's up?' she said, trying to coax it out of me.

'Nothing's wrong. I was just talking with some girls at school and want to get deodorant. They've all got some, and I want some too,' I lied again.

She wasn't having any of it, 'Well, you're kind of young, and don't need—'

'Oh, come on Mom. It's not a big deal, all of the other girls at school put it on after gym,' I cut her off. I was desperate to be like all the other girls.

Still not convinced, but willing to work with me, she said, 'I guess, if you really want to try it. We'll go shopping this weekend.'

I was relieved Mom had agreed, but frustrated at the same time. The deodorant wouldn't fix the source of the smell, but I wouldn't dare mention that. *Why doesn't Mom want to make our house nice and clean? Why won't she do anything?*

We pulled into the garage, and I immediately started a load of laundry. I added extra soap so my clothes would get cleaner and smell better. But there was another problem – where was I going to put my clean clothes once they were dry? Where would they not get stinky?

Neither my mom nor I had a chest of drawers to store clothes, and our closets couldn't be accessed. Mom's was filled with soda bottles, discarded newspapers, old clothes and garbage. Mine, on the other hand, was filled with old toys, old clothes and building materials. The door wouldn't latch, so Mom had put a desk in front of it to stop the contents from falling out.

I didn't want to leave the clothes in the basement because that gave them a mouldy, musty smell, which made me sneeze.

My mom liked to sit on the left side of the couch, and clothes and garbage would pile up on the right side. If I cleared the garbage off, then I would have a clean area to keep my clothes. *They shouldn't smell too much there.*

I grabbed an empty trash bag and got to work on cleaning off the right side of the couch. Watching me with puzzled eyes from the computer chair, my mom asked, 'What are you doing?'

'Just throwing away some crap,' I explained, as I stuffed the garbage bag full.

'Well don't touch that pile there. And, hey, I haven't finished that soda!'

She really hated it when I touched her newspapers. I felt like every bit of rubbish I touched was like a bomb ready to go off. I started picking up around the pile that was off limits. I grabbed takeaway containers that had been festering for ages, and after they were cleared, I stuffed the junk underneath in the trash bag.

As I was stuffing an old, leaky lotion bottle into the bag Mom cleared her throat loudly.

I jumped and looked back at her, still holding on to the bottle. Her lips were pursed, and her brows furrowed. Looking at the bottle, she shook her head 'no'. 'There is still lotion in that.'

Quietly, I put the broken, dirty lotion bottle back on the floor.

Please don't explode, please don't explode.

• • •

I couldn't focus on any of my classes all week because I was worrying about whether I smelt. I isolated myself, staying indoors during break and eating lunch alone. It was embarrassing enough having a teacher tell me I stank, I didn't need my classmates making fun of me for it. The weekend came around and I had to beg Mom to take me to the shops.

'Mom, please can we go to the store now? You promised I could get deodorant.'

'You don't need it right now. We can get it later today or tomorrow. Hell, we can even get it sometime next week,' she snapped.

'But Mom! All of the other girls have some, and I think I might smell.' I pleaded, trying anything to get her to buy me some.

She rolled her eyes and shook her head. 'You don't smell, where did you even get that from? But if you want it that bad, then put your shoes on.'

As fast as lightening, I sprinted for my shoes.

I even grabbed my mom's shoes on the way back to the living room, hoping she would move faster with my help.

• • •

We walked into the store, but my mom headed towards the fruits and vegetables, the opposite direction to the cosmetics aisle.

'Mom, I thought we were getting me deodorant,' I whispered.

'We are, but we're going grocery shopping first. We'll get that on the way out,' she said, picking out bananas.

Groaning, I mumbled, 'Fine, but can we make it quick?'

She stopped in her tracks and glared at me.

'Look, we're here now. We're going to get your goddamn deodorant, but first we need other shit. Let's go,' she pushed me forwards.

I was in awe when we finally rounded the corner for the deodorant aisle. It looked like a rainbow, there were so many different colours of packaging and the whole aisle smelt wonderful.

I finally snapped out of my daze and headed straight for the 'girly' coloured ones. I thought it was going to be easy picking one out, but I was so confused. There was wetness protection, invisible, gel, spray on and clinical strength. It was so much all at once for an eight-year-old to work out. I had to pick a scent that I liked and a strong smell, which would also mask the smell of the house. I settled on a lilac scented deodorant. It had a strong smell, and reminded me of the lilac bushes we had around the house. Lilacs were my favourite flower.

I didn't even wait for the cashier to pack it in the bag. I grabbed it from the conveyer belt and ran to the supermarket bathroom.

'Okay Britney, you've seen Mom do this hundreds of times. How hard can it be?' I muttered under my breath in the cubicle.

Like a present on Christmas day, I unwrapped the packaging, throwing the cellophane on the floor. I popped the top, taking in the smell of the lilac. It smelt like summer. I imagined myself standing in our back yard, surrounded by our lilac bushes, the warmth of the sun touching my skin. Our yard was the only place that was trash free, that seemed like normal small-town Illinois. Well, except for the pit. That was a big hole in our back yard, about 30 feet by 20 feet, filled with weeds, garbage and a whole bunch of other stuff. It had once been a swimming pool, but Mom hadn't taken care of it, and eventually the liner broke. But even there, overgrown trees covered most of the rubbish. For a moment I was happy, not worrying about how I smelt or how I looked.

I heard a toilet flush, and I was swept back into reality. I lifted my shirt and smeared the deodorant on my armpits. I immediately felt better, cleaner. I could be normal when I went back to school on Monday.

• • •

I was awake before the alarm went off. I couldn't wait to go to school. I had my deodorant and my clothes were clean, and they hadn't had much of a chance to pick up the smell of the house.

When the alarm rang, I rolled over and smacked my mom on the arm, 'Mom, it's time to get up.'

'Put it on snooze, I'll get up when it goes off again,' she said, yawning.

I did as I was told and hopped off the bed while my mom repositioned herself. She stretched out like a starfish now that I wasn't sleeping next to her.

That snooze button allowed Mom to sleep in fifteen minutes longer, but it was shower time for me. I washed my hair two times. I was going to smell really good when I got to school.

I applied a thick layer of deodorant under my armpits. *What if I put some on my stomach? Will*

I smell even better? I ran a finger across the stick before running it across my belly and chest. *There, now I smell like lilacs, not this house,* I smiled to myself in the mirror.

I headed to the living room – my new laundry room. I grabbed my clothes off the right arm of the couch. *There isn't any old food next to my clothes, so they shouldn't smell too bad.* I got dressed where I stood, leaving the towel where it fell around me.

I had most of my confidence back at school that day. I could look my teacher in the eyes. I even said 'Hi' to Mr Portsly. I played with my friends during break and ate with them at lunch. I wasn't afraid to raise my hand in class to answer questions.

I watched my classmates' reactions to me and they seemed normal. I sprayed myself during break with the air freshener from the bathroom, just to make sure.

Even though it was a good day, by the end of it, I had a funny feeling in my stomach. Questions kept popping into my head: *Do any of my classmates have to find a clean spot to put their clothes? Do they have to use deodorant and stolen air freshener to mask the smell of their house? I'm just a kid, I shouldn't have to worry about any of this stuff – should I?*

I felt trapped because I couldn't ask them for fear that they would think I was a total freak. At the same time, I couldn't ask my mom, because she got angry when I tried to clear away just some of the rubbish.

I decided it was better just to keep my thoughts locked inside.

CHAPTER 4

'Kiddo. I want to talk with you about something,' Mom said, gripping the steering wheel tightly on the way home from the babysitters one day. 'How do you feel about staying home alone? I think you're mature enough that you can do it.'

A big grin spread across my face. Excited, I said, 'You're going to let me stay home alone?'

'Yes, if you think you're ready, because I sure do,' she replied, nodding her head.

Bouncing excitedly in my seat, I asked, 'When will I be allowed?'

'I have to give the babysitter some notice, let her know you won't be coming anymore. Your last day with her will be the end of this week. You'll go home after school on Monday.'

When we got home I couldn't contain my excitement. I felt so grown up, I was only nine, and Mom trusted me enough to be home alone. She was trying to make it seem like it was not a big deal. 'It'll only be for an hour, maximum. That's not too long.'

I am free. I don't have to listen to Mom or my babysitter anymore. I call the shots. My mom believes that I can handle myself, even if it's just for an hour.

• • •

The next morning, I had to take the bus to school. I was the third stop on the route, so I got to pick pretty much any seat that I wanted. I usually sat in front of Josh. He got on the stop before me.

'Psst, Josh. You awake?' I asked quietly.

Exhaling slowly, he said, 'I guess I am now. What's up?'

'I get to stay home alone after school, starting next Monday,' I boasted.

The bus stopped again, this time at the trailer park. My friend Sandra got on, and sat in the seat across the aisle from me.

'Hey guys, what's up?' she greeted us.

'Britney's just told me that she'll get to start staying home alone next week,' he told her.

Looking concerned, Sandra said, 'Isn't that scary? Your house seems so big when Mom drives past it.'

'Not to mention someone was murdered in your house,' Josh cut in.

Sandra gasped, and quickly scooped up her backpack, hugging it close.

'Oh, shut up Josh,' I snapped. 'No one was murdered in my house.'

'No, I'm serious. You didn't know? One day the guy who lived in the house before you went crazy. He killed his wife, and then shot himself. Wanna know what's messed up though?' he asked with a smirk.

Sandra was whimpering in her seat, her hands clamped over her ears.

'What?' I asked him.

He looked around for a second, then leaned in closer, and whispered, 'They had a daughter. She got home from school as usual, but when she went inside, she found both of her parents, dead.'

Waves of fear cascaded down my back. I became aware that it was cold and very dark outside. *This can't be real*, I thought, trying to reassure myself.

With a smirk on his face, Josh taunted, 'Go ahead, ask your mom.'

Mike, a fifth grader who was sitting behind Sandra, pitched in, 'You know Britney, Josh isn't lying. A murder-suicide happened in your house.'

I didn't know what to say, so I turned around and faced forward. I didn't talk to anyone for the remainder of the bus ride. *Mom would have told me about this if it was true and, besides, she wouldn't want to live in a house where someone was murdered.* I tried to make myself feel better.

All day, all I could think about was what Josh had said. Echoing through my head, 'Someone was murdered in your house!', I couldn't focus on anything.

Later that evening, I was sitting on a beanbag watching TV. It was uncomfortable because it was resting on a few bags of trash that we hadn't thrown away that week.

I couldn't get what Josh had said out of my mind, but I didn't know how to ask my mom about it. I kept peeking over at her. *How could she just sit happily, knowing someone was murdered here? Does she even know? What if she gets mad at me for asking?* Over the noise of the TV, I heard some creaks coming from downstairs.

I was scared.

'Mom, was somebody murdered here?' I blurted out. My hands were shaking.

Sighing deeply, she asked, 'Where did you hear that?'

'Josh told me someone murdered their wife, then killed himself. Then someone else said it was true. A murder-suicide happened here.'

Staring at the ground, massaging her temples, she explained, 'They were right. It happened a while before I moved in here. The real estate agents couldn't sell the house because of what happened. I made a very low offer, and they accepted it. They must have been desperate to sell, and I got a great deal.'

The air stood still, and everything fell quiet. The walls started closing in on me. 'What, what do you mean?' I stammered. 'People actually died here? Where did they die?' I scanned the room for signs of someone dying.

'Well, the husband shot his wife in our room, and he killed himself in the bathtub.' She said, shrugging like it was no big deal.

'He killed her in our room? The room we sleep in? That doesn't scare you?' I asked, my body shaking with fear.

'It's no big deal. It happened a few years before I moved in. It got cleaned up, everything is fine,' she replied, annoyed.

I couldn't sleep a wink that night. My heart raced every time I heard a noise. The sound of the mice scratching around our bedroom was ten times louder than usual. I imagined the horrible things that had gone on our house.

My heart pounded between my ears. *Boom, boom, boom.*

• • •

After a long week of waiting, Monday finally arrived. I'd tried to push the images of the murder to the back of my mind. I'd become good at blanking things out – like how messy our house was. Instead, I tried to get myself excited about the fact I was going to be home alone for the first time. I had to get a note signed by my mom saying I could be dropped off at home without her having to wait for me at the bus stop. I then had to get that note signed by the principal. She looked over the note carefully and drew a deep breath before speaking.

'I usually get these kinds of notes from fifth graders. It's good to see a fourth grader who is mature enough to handle being home alone.'

I smiled. It felt good having other adults think I was grown up.

I was super giddy the entire day, telling everyone my news. All of my friends and classmates were jealous because I was the first one out of all of them to stay home alone. No one else's parents trusted them enough.

School ended and I headed up to the bus queue. I stood tall and proud, and I couldn't keep a big grin off my face. My bus driver opened the door and I hopped up the steps, enthusiastically handing her my note. Giving it a quick glance, she said, 'Your mom called me earlier to let me know what's up. Be careful when you're home, okay?'

'Oh, I will,' I said, still smiling as I found my usual seat.

Josh got on a while later and sat behind me. My heart sank.

'First day home alone, huh? You're not worried about getting spooked by their ghosts,' he taunted.

My chest tightened, and I stopped breathing for a second. I hadn't thought about ghosts.

'Josh, stop it! You're just jealous I get to stay home alone and you don't,' I snapped. I wanted him to stop.

Putting a hand on my shoulder, he said, 'I'm sorry Britney. I was only joking – well, about the ghosts, not the murder. You know that part is true.'

Boom, boom, boom, my heart started racing again.

'Don't talk to me anymore Josh,' I whimpered.

I now wanted the bus ride to last forever. *The ghosts of that guy and his wife might be haunting my house. I've never seen them before, but I've also never been home alone.*

Before I knew it, I could see my house through the trees that surrounded it. I felt sick with nerves.

Maybe I can ask the bus driver to not drop me off, to keep going. But where would she take me?

The bus stopped. I had to get off.

My chest was tight, and my hands were shaking. I slowly walked down the bus aisle. All of a sudden the horn honked, loud and long. I nearly jumped out of my skin.

'Sorry hon, someone didn't stop for my stop sign,' the bus driver explained.

I was a bag of nerves.

I hopped off and walked to the porch. I sat at the patio table for a while, building up the courage to go inside. After what seemed like an eternity, I finally got up and went to the door. I peeked inside the window to make sure everything was okay.

'Well, everything looks normal,' I muttered, taking a deep breath.

I unlocked the door, pushing it wide open. I took another look before entering the house. I gingerly tiptoed my way up the stairs, checking over my shoulder the entire time. Each step creaked like an animal taking its last breath.

I got to the top and quickly slammed the door behind me. I hooked the chain lock across and collapsed on the floor, breathing heavily, my heart racing. I'd always hated our stairs, but today they were even scarier.

On the way to the couch in the living room, I grabbed the phone. Mom said if I didn't call her when I got home I'd be in trouble. The phone started ringing in my hand. She had just beaten me to it.

'Hi Mom, I'm home,' I said.

'Hi kiddo, how does it feel being home alone?' she asked.

'Good, I just grabbed a snack. I'm going to watch TV, then do homework,' I said confidently, so she wouldn't question whether or not I could handle myself.

'That's good. Well, I have to get back to work. If you've got any problems just call me. Okay?'

'Okay Mom. Bye.' I hung up.

Just grow up. There aren't any ghosts trying to hurt you. The murder happened a long time ago, everything is okay. Do what you told Mom you were going to do.

I found a show that I wanted to watch then went to get myself a snack. As I opened the fridge, I was hit by a wave of stench. It smelt like rotting flesh. We usually cleaned the fridge out once a month, but things like milk jugs stayed in there for months. Some stuff had been in there so long it had fused to the shelves and I couldn't identify what the hell it was. It was second nature to me to only eat unopened packets or food that Mom had just brought home. This time I settled for some crisps.

I returned to the living room to watch TV. I was still a little bit nervous, but I kept telling myself that everything was okay. When my show was finished, I turned off the TV so I could concentrate on my homework.

It was always hard doing my homework because I didn't have a clean table to rest on. I had to balance all my work on the arm of the couch. I had only been working on my multiplication for a few minutes when the room got colder and I heard the stairs downstairs creaking. My heart started beating a thousand times a second. I could hear it pounding in my ears. I felt paralysed with fear, and strained to look at the door from the corners of my eyes. *I put the chain lock on, I know I did*, I calmed myself slightly.

The stairs stopped creaking, but I was still too petrified to move. All of a sudden I heard something rustling on the other side of the wall – in my mom's bedroom.

Oh no, that's where he shot her. He knows I'm home alone now. I reached for the phone and dialled my mom's work number.

Stop. Don't call her, you're being silly. She'll think you're too young to stay home alone if you bother her with ghost stories.

I sat back down and continued working on my homework.

Even though I kept trying to tell myself everything was all right, and there was nothing to worry about, I was still so jumpy. I couldn't focus on my calculations any longer. I checked the time. It could be thirty minutes before Mom got home. It was starting to get dark outside and I could still hear some noises downstairs. I was so scared, I just wanted her home.

Maybe I'll feel safer if I keep an eye out for Mom?

I ran to the kitchen as that was the only room from where I could see the road that Mom would be driving up. Damn it, I was too short to look out the window. I ran back to the living room to get the computer chair. It was buried amongst a pile of trash so high, it reached the bottom of the seat. The more I was being slowed down by rubbish, the more anxious I felt. I lifted it up over full garbage bags and stacks of newspapers. My arms were hurting, but I ignored the pain, if I dragged the chair instead then wrappers and bottles would get caught on the legs, bringing more trash along with it.

Something big and black suddenly ran across my path.

Oh my God, my heart was in my mouth. I needed to get to high ground. *Run Britney, run.*

It took every last ounce of energy to run with the chair to the kitchen. I placed it in front of the window, climbed on top and waited for Mom to come home. Every pair of headlights that sliced through the darkness brought hope that it might be her.

The chair had a grey plastic upholstery that was cracked and falling apart. The yellow filling inside was rotting, making my feet super itchy. I was scared to move though, and tried to blank out the itching and the moaning stairs, and the thought that there may be some big black creature hiding in the trash.

As soon as I saw my mom's car pass under the street light, I hopped off the chair, falling onto the ground because my legs were so stiff. The floor was tacky, like a used sticker. So many things had been dropped or splashed on the carpet that you couldn't tell what its original colour was anymore. Good thing I fell on some plastic bags, only my hand touched the floor. I stood up and wiped my palm across my trouser legs.

I ran to the door, undid the chain lock and threw it open. I was safe from almost anything once my mom got home. I wasn't afraid of the basement or the sounds anymore.

I was already at the bottom of the stairs when the garage door opened. I hopped down the last few steps into the basement, tripping over some laundry. I waited patiently in the doorway for her to turn the car off. I was not allowed to be in the garage if there was a running car in there. As soon as the engine cut out, I ran to my mom and opened her door.

'Hi Mom,' I squealed, hugging her tightly.

She pushed me away.

'Don't hang on me. I feel gross after working today,' she dismissed me.

I awkwardly pulled away my hands and looked at the floor. I could never understand why one moment she liked me, and the next she didn't.

'Oh, okay. I'm just glad you're home,' I said quietly.

Mom grunted and slammed the car door shut.

'Mom, I saw some big black animal running around near the kitchen,' I confessed.

'Oh jeez, the rats are back,' she shrugged.

CHAPTER 5

Mom had been collecting newspapers and coupons ever since I could remember, but things took a turn one weekend.

After church one Sunday morning, we headed to our usual spot – the gas station down the road. Mom normally bought a coffee with a bunch of flavourings added, and I'd get a hot chocolate with all of the marshmallows I could sprinkle on top.

We both entered the gas station. I immediately went to the hot drink machine and my mom went over to grab the paper. Before I'd even taken a cup, Mom screeched my name across the store.

'We're leaving!' she yelled, urgently.

'But why? We haven't even got our drinks,' I said, confused.

Her eyes were wild with a look of crazed panic. 'They don't have the newspaper. Let's go.' She ran for the door.

I shuffled out of the gas station, and hopped in the car. We then went to the liquor store across the street from our house. They too were sold out. My mom was now angry.

'I just want the fucking paper,' she thumped the steering wheel with her fists.

Why was Mom getting so angry about a newspaper? I started to tremble; I didn't like it when Mom got mad over something I didn't understand.

We drove to two more places, but without joy. Mom's driving and her temper were getting increasingly erratic. I clung onto the car seat because I was afraid we might crash.

'Mom, I don't mind if I don't read the comics today,' I mumbled, trying to get her to slow down.

'Well I do mind. I want my fucking paper.'

I pushed myself back into the car seat, like a crab into its shell. I didn't get out this time, as Mom checked the fourth store. After a few minutes she reappeared, clutching the Sunday newspaper. She had a look of extreme relief on her face. I was relieved too. Her anger was over and we could go home.

As soon as Mom came in the door, she peeled her sweaty clothes off her body, and let them drop to the floor. She kicked the trash out of her path and flopped onto the couch. She opened the paper.

Every time she turned a page she had to tug the paper from her sticky legs.

I sat quietly on the stool next to the left arm of the couch. That was now my corner, my space, which I kept clean. The stool was black with gold flowers embroidered on the top. The edge had black silk scalloped on the side, with decorative black and gold rope beautifully woven through it. To top it off, it had five black feather tassels evenly spaced around it. If my mom was home, that was my seat now. I didn't like sitting on the couch itself so much anymore because Mom would leave sweat and other marks on the leather.

I watched cartoons on the TV while Mom started looking through the coupons. The ones she wanted to use she'd put in a pile. I wondered why she did that. She would never look at them again; she just seemed to want to collect coupons.

• • •

Mom's mood swings got worse after that weekend. One minute she liked me, the next I wasn't good enough. In the morning she would cuddle me, in the evening she would scream and shout, inches from my face. The list of chores she gave me to do when I got home from school seemed to get bigger every day. She now was ordering me to throw away the trash, even though she was collecting more rubbish than ever. I felt like I was walking on eggshells, trying not to upset her.

It was the middle of the school week, and I was feeling overwhelmed. The front door opened, I stopped what I was doing and craned my ear.

'Hi kiddo, I'm home,' said Mom, closing the door behind her.

'Hi Mom,' I yelled back.

She started clunking up the stairs. I could hear plastic grocery bags rustling with each step she took. When she was upstairs, she dumped some already burnt candles and dusty fake flowers from work and started firing questions: 'I thought I said to pick up five bags of trash, and how many loads of laundry have you done? What about the dishes? You're still working on homework?'

I didn't make eye contact with her because I knew she'd have a look of disappointment on her face.

'I'm still working on homework. I picked up three bags of trash, and the first load is drying and a second load is being washed right now. I haven't started on dishes,' I said, feeling under attack.

She threw her hands up in the air, shaking her head. 'Are you serious? What the hell have you been doing this entire time?'

I looked at the floor in front of the couch, holding my breath.

'Well, what have you been doing?'

Her eyes widened like saucers in anger. I wanted to take back my words.

'I ... I said I have a lot of homework. I even have more ...' I stuttered.

She grabbed my backpack, and tore through my folders, looking for my work.

'What did you have as homework today?' she barked.

I shuffled all of the homework I'd completed into a small pile, and handed it to her. I then rifled through my backpack and found the work I still needed to complete. Sometimes I had a lot, and sometimes I didn't have any.

'See, I had a lot of homework today,' I said, handing her the incomplete work.

'Well, you had a lot of chores today too,' she said, snatching the papers out of my hand.

Mom sat down at the computer desk and fingered through all of my work.

'This shouldn't have taken you more than half an hour. There is no excuse as to why your chores aren't done,' she said. 'I think you're just being lazy.' She tossed my homework back at me.

I was now feeling terrified about asking for her help on my next project. I nervously played with the corners of my math book. *Should I ask her or not? If I ask her, will she shout at me? If I don't, the teacher will shout at me.*

'I need something to colour this,' I said, gingerly holding out a math graph.

'We don't have anything for you to colour this with,' she snapped. 'When you were little, you were lazy, and you wouldn't take care of your coloured pencils. So now you don't get them.'

'I'm sorry,' I mumbled. I could feel the prickles of tears starting to sting. 'I don't remember doing it, but I'm sorry anyway. Can we please go to the store and get some coloured pencils so I can finish this?' I begged.

Mom let out a horrific cackle.

'No, didn't you hear anything I just said? You didn't pick up after yourself then, so I'm not going to waste money on something that you're not going to take care of.'

'Then what am I going to do about my homework? It's due tomorrow,' I panicked, my voice breaking for fear of failing the assignment.

'I guess I'll just have to bring you in early so you can use your teacher's coloured pencils. That's what they're there for,' she shrugged me off.

I couldn't sleep that night for fear of failing. *I'm a failure. I can't do anything right.*

• • •

I would never normally go to my teacher's room before school started. I'd play in the playground or hang out in the library where they had board games. The hallway was dark, but I could see my classroom door was shut. *Maybe Mr Portsly is here and just wants to keep his door closed?* I reached for the doorknob, turned the handle and it swung open.

'Mr Portsly?' I called out.

Looking up from his desk with a startled face, he said, 'Oh, hi Britney. How can I help you?'

I put my backpack on my desk and pulled out the incomplete homework sheet.

'Can I use some of the coloured pencils to finish my homework? I don't have any at home,' I asked.

'No problem,' he said, pointing to the craft rack. 'You know, you could have just used crayons or markers. The paper says coloured pencils, but it doesn't matter what you use as long as it's coloured.'

'I don't have anything to colour with at home,' I said, picking out pretty colours.

Awkwardly, adjusting himself in his chair, he said, 'Um, you don't have things to colour with?

Markers? Crayons? Coloured pencils? Nothing?'

Shrugging my shoulders, I said, 'No, my mom said they would just get lost, so she wasn't going to waste the money on them. She told me I can just use the ones at school. That's what they're there for.'

Mr Portsly rummaged around in his desk. After a few moments, he put a new ten pack of coloured pencils on my desk.

'Just keep these in your backpack, only take them out at home if you need them for school. Okay?' He patted my back.

I smiled. I could feel his warmth and kindness.

The bell rang, and everyone rushed inside from the playground and settled behind their desks.

'All right everyone, quiet down,' Mr Portsly said.

'The spelling test on Friday is being moved up to tomorrow.'

Everyone in class started moaning and protesting. Talking over us, he continued, 'I know it's short notice, but you're going to have a substitute teacher Thursday and Friday.'

My heart started racing. I panicked. I wasn't going to have enough time to do my chores and prepare for the test. But if I didn't score well, my mom would get mad at me. I snatched my spelling words out of my desk and scanned over them.

When I got home after school, I called my mom like usual.

'Hi Mom, I'm home,' I checked in.

'Hi kiddo. I need you to pick up seven bags of trash, wash my blankets and some work clothes, and if you could rake the yard that would be great,' she ordered.

'Well, the spelling test got moved to ...' I tried to explain.

'I have to go, I'm really busy. Love ya, bye.' She cut me off and hung up.

Putting the phone down, I looked at the living room, trying to pick out what trash I could throw away. She would get very angry if I touched her coupons or newspapers. Sighing deeply, I headed to our bedroom.

I dreaded what I was about to find.

We used to have sheets and pillowcases and all the sorts of bedding I'd seen at my friends' houses. That had stopped since Mom started wetting the bed.

Because she was so big, my mom had a hard time getting up in the middle of the night to go to the bathroom. Most nights she now wet the bed. Sometimes, she did it more than once. I made sure to sleep on the very edge of the bed, so she didn't get me and my blankets wet too. I hated the feeling of waking up in the sticky mess. It was cold by the morning and clung to me like glue.

It had been a few days since her blankets had been washed, so most of them were wet. I stood at the end of the bed, staring at the crater in the middle. My mom had peed so much that the springs under her had rusted and disintegrated, leaving a large dip. I pulled off all of her blankets and tossed them into the crater, which was covered with the largest blanket.

Carefully, trying to avoid the wet parts, I dragged the mass of blankets off the bed. They dropped to the floor with a squishy thud, spraying my ankles with cold pee. I yelped and ran to the bathroom, hopped in the bathtub and rinsed off my legs. I regained my composure, dried off and went back to our room.

The smell was the first thing to hit me as I entered the door. It was so strong and musty that my throat closed up and my eyes started watering. Taking a step back, I pulled my shirt up over my nose and took a few quick breaths. I grabbed the corner of the bottom blanket and dragged the pile of blankets down the hallway to the upstairs door. There was a trail of pee from our room, like a trail of slime behind a slug.

Shaking my head in disgust, my shirt slid off my nose. I wasn't expecting it and got a deep breath of her urine. The smell was so strong, it stung. Shutting my eyes as tight as I could, I dropped the blanket and tried pretending I wasn't drowning in pee. I imagined I was standing on a tropical beech, hiking up mountains or even at Disney World, the happiest place on Earth – but nothing worked. Every pissy breath I took hurtled me back to my reality.

I opened the upstairs door, kicking the blankets into the basement. They got caught halfway down the stairs on some books and clothes. My foot landed in a puddle as I stepped down. I was confused as to where the water came from, but shrugged it off, and continued downstairs. I jumped over the pile of blankets so I could grab them from below. I stopped in my tracks. There was a stream of pee flowing down the stairs because the blankets were so saturated. Suddenly it dawned on me – I didn't step in a puddle of water, I stepped in a puddle of urine. Fed up with her blankets, I yanked them down, dodging them so I didn't get sprayed again.

I wrapped my hands in my mom's dirty work clothes so I could stuff the blankets into the washer without touching her pee. I could only fit two blankets into the washer at a time, so I had two more loads after this. I started the load and headed back upstairs, avoiding the rivers and puddles.

Once upstairs, I grabbed a box of trash bags and flipped on the TV. My favourite show was just starting. *Okay, pick up as many bags of trash as possible while this is on. Once it's done, it should be time to hang out the laundry, then I'll study for the spelling test and finish my homework.*

Sitting in a nest of garbage, I started grabbing anything in reach. A pizza box with grease stains, Reese's Peanut Butter Cup wrappers, a Tupperware bowl with God knows what growing inside. I came across some clothes, which I could throw away because they had holes chewed through them. *Have the rats been eating the clothes?*

I filled the first bag and set it next to the upstairs door. I was making good progress because the first advert break hadn't played yet. I sat on the couch and started re-stacking the newspaper piles. If I grabbed the newspaper on top, my mom would know it was missing because it was fresh in her head. If I took newspapers from the bottom of the pile, however, she wouldn't know and she wouldn't yell at me. I filled almost a whole bag just re-stacking the piles.

After the second bag was full, I started picking up the garbage in front of the TV. Due to her obesity, it was hard for my mom to climb over the trash, so she didn't know what was in front of the TV. That meant I could throw all of it away without her getting angry with me.

Clothes I'd never seen before appeared as I sorted through it all, stained and chewed. Shoes that had been separated from their partner long ago were buried under old late payment bills and fast food wrappers. I picked up a tattered old cracker box and found some pictures I had once drawn, ruined. They were from kindergarten and first grade. The corners had been chewed on by mice and they had water stains, which had made the pictures bleed.

I bit my lip but I couldn't stop myself from crying as I shoved my drawings in the trash bag. *She doesn't care about me. Grandma and Aunt Maxine keep pictures on their fridges or hanging on the wall. Mom just lets my stuff get ruined. My special creations are nothing more than trash.*

There were eight minutes of my show left and I had five bags of trash picked up. Starting on my sixth bag, I picked up some more ruined clothes to uncover – another full trash bag. I shook my head in disbelief. *Wow, there was a bag of trash buried under more trash. Well, at least the seventh bag is already full.*

I heaved the last two bags of trash to the stairs and tossed them down to the basement. The puddles of pee had evaporated, but I was still cautious as to where I stepped. I changed the laundry, this time successful at not getting my hands covered. I headed back upstairs, and started on my homework.

I heard the downstairs door open, pushing aside the bags of trash in front of it. My heart started racing. *Oh no, is the washer still running? I'm going to get in trouble if it's not.*

'Hi kiddo, I'm home,' Mom yelled. 'I see the yard hasn't been raked,' she added.

I leapt up and opened the upstairs door, straining to hear the washer.

'I'm working on homework and studying for my spelling test. It got moved to tomorrow,' I said. Relaxing when I heard the faint rhythmic whirring of the washer, I added, 'I ... I got seven bags picked up though.' I hoped that was enough.

'Yeah, but laundry isn't done, so I don't have clean work clothes yet, and the yard isn't raked,' she berated me, taking her dirty clothes off. She kicked her clothes into the laundry room and started up the stairs, naked.

'I started laundry right after I hung up with you. I can't make the washer go any faster. I have to study for my spelling test, it's now tomorrow,' I said, with a bit of attitude.

Furrowing her eyebrows, she snapped, 'Don't you talk to me like that.'

She grabbed my arm tightly. 'You know, I get it. You fuck around until there's fifteen minutes till I get home. Then you run around like a chicken with its head cut off doing a half-assed job of all of your chores. You really need to quit being lazy, I don't ask too much of you,' she shouted, inches from my face. I could feel little drops of spit spraying my skin.

My chest was tight, I was so afraid of her. She was red in the face and breathing heavily. Standing there naked, her large belly jiggled with every breath she took. Her hair was pulled back into a ponytail, which was starting to come undone after a long day of work. She looked crazy.

She let me go and brushed past my trembling body to sit on the computer chair. I quickly gathered my homework and went to our bedroom. Turning the volume on the TV up, I started crying. Her hand print was still a faint pink on my arm. It was too hard studying for my spelling test after what happened so I just lay on the edge of the bed, and cried.

I don't know how much time had passed when my stomach started growling like a bear. *Has she*

calmed down enough that I can ask for food?
I rolled off the bed and went to the living room.
Mom was on the computer, browsing the internet.

'Mom, what did you bring to eat?' I asked,
nervously.

She didn't look up to speak to me.

'I served spaghetti and broccoli today. It's on the
couch,' she muttered.

Like an animal I scurried over to the couch,
grabbed the food and started running back to
our bedroom. Something caught my eye. I spotted
the dining table, and wished I could eat there. The
table was covered with stacks of newspapers that
had fallen over. Old candle stubs lay on their sides,
their wax coating any table I could see. Books
were haphazardly thrown into the mix, along with
clothes. All of it lay festering under a thick coat of
dust.

I was so sick of having to find a spot to eat
my food. It was hard trying to balance a couple
of plates and bowls on the arm of the couch or on
the bed. I just wanted to be like a normal family,
to be able to eat a home-cooked meal at the dinner
table. Instead I got the leftovers of whatever she
cooked at work, and I had to search for a clean
place to eat.

I carried my food into our bedroom, wishing things could be different.

• • •

I woke up to the alarm, at 6.30 a.m. Fumbling for the button, I finally pressed 'snooze'. *I must have fallen asleep after I ate*, I thought to myself, sitting up. Mom was next to me on the right.

I hopped off, and started getting ready for school.

Mom didn't have to go to work until later so she gave me a ride. In the car, she asked, 'Are you ready for your spelling test?'

'I hope so. I studied for a while last night,' I said.

'Well you better be, there's no excuse for bad grades.'

I didn't know how to respond, I'd tried so hard to study around my list of chores. Instead I sat quietly, like a lame dog. We pulled up to the school gates, and there were tall pine trees, dotted throughout the grounds. Past the playgrounds and soccer fields, the trees became a dense forest.

The car pulled in, and I was about to climb out when my mom grabbed my shoulder.

'Have a good day. Good luck with your test,' she said, and then let go.

I slammed the car door just as the bell rang. We had cut it close. I walked into the classroom and hung up my backpack at my cubby hole. I sat down and grabbed a copy of my spelling words to get in some last minute study time before the test. Mr Portsly made the announcements for the day; I ignored him and continued studying.

From out of nowhere, Mr Portsly lurched forward and snatched the spelling words out of my hands.

'We're starting the test now.' He spoke quietly, placing the blank test on my desk.

'Oh, sorry,' I whispered, rummaging through my backpack until I found a pencil. We were given thirty words to practise, but only twenty of those would be called out. I knew it wasn't going to be random, the hard words were always chosen.

Mr Portsly announced the first word, and it was an easy one, 'holiday'. *Maybe this won't be so bad*, I thought to myself, scribbling down the word. The next few words flew by with a breeze. But then Mr Portsly said a word I didn't recognise, 'coyote'. I focused on the word, slowly sounding it out. I hadn't finished that word when the next one gushed out. The words were firing out, and before I knew it, the test was over. I looked down to see what I had written, there were gaps everywhere like a crossword. It was my fault – I hadn't spent enough time studying my words. I knew I'd failed the test.

The rest of the day went by in a panicked blur. Too soon it was home time. Mr Portsly stood by the door, handing our tests back as we left for the day. There was a big red 'D' scrawled at the top of mine. My heart galloped as my mom's voice echoed in my head: 'There's no excuse for bad grades.'

I couldn't bring myself to pick up the phone to call my mom when I got home. Eventually, though, I lifted the receiver, and dialled my way to my punishment.

'Hi Mom. I'm home,' I said.

'Hi kiddo. How did you do on your test?' she asked, not missing a beat.

'Um, I got a D,' I said quietly.

'I can't believe it,' she angrily choked on her words. 'You don't get to watch TV for the rest of the week and you're getting extra chores. I need all of the laundry done, seven more bags of trash, and the leaves need to be raked.'

'Okay,' I said meekly.

I quickly got a load of laundry going, and then started on raking the leaves. Cleaning the house was like a never-ending cycle. There was decades of trash all over our house, and it would take years to clean up. I couldn't do it alone. I felt helpless.

I can't seem to do anything right. I can't get chores done and I'm slipping in school. I just want her to be happy with me. I'm a waste of space.

I was starting to hate myself.

Done with the yard, I changed the laundry and started another load. I headed upstairs, straight for our bedroom. *The trash is as high as the bed, I'll knock out seven bags in no time*, I thought, defiantly.

I was sick of being pushed onto the trash in the middle of the night by my mom, so I targeted all of the trash right next to the bed. I had four bags filled before I could see a sliver of the floor. 'Huh, I didn't know our room was carpeted!' I exclaimed. I cleared a mouldy pizza box to find two stacks of newspapers.

Amusing myself, I started reading some of the articles. I saw an ad for a VCR player on sale for $75. I thought that was odd because we had just bought a DVD player a little while ago for only $50. I checked the date that the newspaper was printed. What the hell? The paper was ten years old, a year older than me.

I threw the paper across the room and started kicking the trash around me. I burst out crying. Through the tears I grabbed a dirty drinking glass, and threw it against the far wall. I felt better when it shattered. *She won't even know*, I thought to myself, smashing another glass at the wall.

This isn't even my mess. I didn't put this crap here. I was so mad at my mom for making me clean up the trash she'd left from before I was even born. I wanted to stop doing my chores and tell her how I felt. But although I was angry, I was afraid if I did that she'd abandon me. If she left, I'd have nothing. I'd be all alone in the house where people had been murdered, surrounded by rubbish.

I would rather be treated badly than be alone.

CHAPTER 6

I stared at the phone like it was a bomb ready to blow. My heart raced and my chest was tight. I didn't want to call my mom. For weeks now, every time I called she gave me more chores than I could handle and yelled at me about my grades. I was trying my best, but I was only nine years old – I couldn't manage both.

Slicing the silence, the phone rang.

Mom yelled as soon as I picked up the receiver. 'What the fuck? You usually call about a half hour ago. What the fuck took so long?'

Flinching from the phone, I lied, 'My key dropped under the porch and I had to find it. Then I started a load of laundry. Sorry.'

'You are so irresponsible. Maybe I should send you back to a babysitter. God, I can't believe you. I need you to pick up that pile of shit in the living room, and I need work clothes clean for tomorrow,' she barked, and then hung up.

I kicked her work clothes down the stairs, catching a pile of books along with it. I stacked the books back up but it was pointless really. Every load of laundry tossed down the stairs always managed to snag at least one book. When I tried moving them, Mom got mad. She never said why, but she wanted them to stay on the stairs. She never read them, they just sat there collecting dust until a rogue shirt snagged them. I put her clothes in the washer, headed back upstairs and started picking up the pile of garbage in the living room.

Tears ran down my cheeks.

I cried every time I was picking up garbage now. I couldn't help it. I was so unhappy. I felt like Cinderella from the fairy tale – imprisoned in a house full of rubbish, made to do chores while my friends were outside playing.

Maybe my mom will clean up after herself if I'm not here to do it, I thought, throwing a mangled shoe into the bag.

'There, the "pile of shit" is picked up,' I shouted, tossing the bag by the door leading to the basement.

I couldn't see through the tears now. Every inch of my body was screaming in anger and pain. Knowing I would get in trouble for filling just one bag, I started scouting for another place to pick up.

There was a bunch of stuff behind the couch that separated the living room in half. Hunched over, I tossed the pile of garbage to one side. I unearthed an empty pack of old cigarettes and broke down, falling to my knees. *This isn't fair. This is my mom's mess. She quit smoking years ago and I'm still finding empty packs.* I sobbed.

Through the tears, I kept shovelling trash into the bag. Every handful brought out a deeper sob. I couldn't take it anymore. I fell against the back of the couch, my face in my hands and howled.

'I can't do this anymore,' I shouted at nothing. 'I don't *want* to do this anymore.'

People commit suicide all the time. The thought popped into my head.

I started thinking it on repeat, trying to calm myself down. I peeled myself off the sticky floor and walked to the kitchen. There was a knife on the floor next to the oven. I picked it up, and headed to the sink to wash it off. I went back to the living room and sat on the couch, clasping the knife so tightly my knuckles turned white.

Tears welled in my eyes as I placed the knife on my wrist. *Finally, all of this will be over.* I let out a sigh of relief. Pressing down on my skin, I pulled the knife, slowly, deliberately, across my wrist.

Nothing happened. It didn't even hurt. I ran the pad of my thumb across the blade – only to find out it was completely blunt. I threw the knife across the room. *Nothing works in this house!* Running to the kitchen, I desperately searched for another one.

It's no use, you know there isn't another one, I thought, giving up my quest in frustration.

Racking my brain, I contemplated other means of suicide. *I don't know how to hang myself, how would I tie the noose?* My eyes scanned the living room, and latched on the one thing we did have – trash bags. *I'll suffocate myself.*

It seemed fitting. I walked over to the box of bags.

I crumpled to the floor and pulled a trash bag out of the box. Slowly, I opened it and slid my head into a corner of the bag. I tightly tied it around my neck, snug. I laid back, closed my eyes and waited for the stress to stop.

After a few minutes, I realized dying was going to take a lot longer than I had initially thought. *That's okay, I can't deal with this life anymore, just wait it out.* I curled up in the foetal position. There was a soda bottle poking me in the side, so I readjusted myself, but I couldn't get comfortable. I just wanted to die in comfort.

Tears pooled in the bag next to my face, matting my hair to my cheeks. No matter how much I adjusted myself I couldn't get comfortable. A food wrapper was scratching my legs, a dirty bowl was poking into my side and some old string tickled my toes.

Suddenly, the room started going black around the edges. My breath quickened. *Is this it? Will it all stop soon?* I squirmed on the nest of trash.

My head was spinning. My vision tunnelled and it got to the point that I couldn't see much. I started gagging, and with each retch I saw less and less.

I pushed myself up, trying to stop the gagging. *I didn't think this is how it would go. This isn't peaceful. It's painful.*

The retching stopped as I leaned against the back of the couch. I panted through the plastic. I felt trash at my feet and I kicked it in anger. *Get it away from me.* I grabbed handfuls of garbage on either side of me and threw it into the dark. I panicked and tore a hole in the trash bag near my mouth. I sucked in a big, long breath.

I toppled to my side on the exposed carpet and sobbed.

I want to die, but not in a pile of garbage. I'm a coward.

Crushed, the thought came unbidden to my mind: *Would Mom even find me?*

• • •

After what seemed like forever, I calmed down enough to stand. I tore the bag off my head and shoved it into the trash bag with all the other rubbish. Tears were trickling down my face as I carried on filling the bag. I tossed it next to the upstairs door on my way to our bedroom.

I curled into a ball on the bed and waited for Mom to get home. Minutes later, I heard the door open.

'I'm home,' she shouted up the stairs. I didn't respond, I just lay there like a dead animal.

The door to the washer slammed shut with a *boom.*

'I thought I said I needed work clothes for tomorrow. Why the fuck aren't they in the dryer?' she angrily yelled, charging up the stairs like a rhinoceros.

She slammed the living room door against the wall.

'Where the fuck are you?' There was a pause as she surveyed the living room. '*And* you only picked up two bags of trash. Jesus Christ, you're lazy,' she went on.

CHAPTER 6

I hate you, I hate you, I hate you. I hate myself.

She charged around the corner, and stood in the doorway of our room. She was almost as wide as the door. Even though she was a few feet away, she seemed to loom over me. She started yelling, but I wasn't paying attention to what she was saying. I was thinking how much I hated her. I wanted my old mom back, the mom who didn't make me do chores.

She wore her maroon shirt; it had stains all down the front. Her black trousers had flour ground into them from where she'd wipe her hands off. Her hair was in a matted pony tail, her second chin jiggled every time she opened her mouth. She didn't ever groom, so her eyebrows were thick and wild as she furrowed them in anger.

She kicked the bed, startling me.

'Did you hear anything I just fucking said?' she asked, her fists balled at her side.

I slowly lifted my head off the dirty bed.

'I've thrown up a couple of times. I don't feel good,' I lied. I finished my sentence off with a fake gag.

Like a flick of a switch, my mom's anger dissolved and she sat at the foot of the bed, stroking my leg.

I couldn't cope with her mood swings – it was too much.

'Oh, kiddo. I'm sorry. I didn't know you weren't feeling good. Good news though, I happened to bring soup home. We had chicken noodle today at the hospital.'

'No thanks, I just want to lie down,' I said, weakly. I felt beaten.

Patting my leg, she said, 'Okay hon. We'll see how you're feeling in the morning. If you still feel sick, I'll take you to Grandma's house.'

She got up and headed to the kitchen.

I scooped my blanket over me, wrapping my body up tightly. The moon was bright that night. I looked at it through the window, and tears slipped down the side of my face.

Maybe it'll get better, I tried to reassure myself. *Maybe.*

PART 2

CHAPTER 7

I had only a few days left of my summer break. I cranked the knob to the blue side and waited until I felt the cold water run over my body. There's nothing more satisfying than ending a shower with cold water when the weather is hot.

I picked at the rotting linoleum wall to pass time as I waited for my body to drip-dry. I drew pictures on the exposed plasterboard with wet fingers. Smiley faces were my favourite thing. I barely had to touch it for it to slough off. There was a yellow film that lined the inside of the bathtub. Where there was still linoleum, mildew flourished. I could see bare pipes through holes that had formed in the plasterboard. I could see the basement through the pipes.

Finally I was dry enough so I slid back the shower curtain, and stepped out. I kicked the dirty clothes pile until I saw a towel. Mom said we didn't need to wash towels after we used them because we were using them to dry off our clean bodies.

I wrapped up in the musty towel and went to the living room to see what Mom was doing. She was sitting at the computer, naked. Her belly was hanging in between her thighs, wiggling with each breath she took. I propped myself on the arm of the couch, straining to see what was on the computer screen.

The towel was small and didn't cover me well, so the front opened when I sat down.

'What are you doing?' I asked.

'Just playing Sudoku. Want to help?' she asked, turning to look at me.

'Yeah, sure. You can put a ...' I leaned in to see the screen.

Mom narrowed her eyes and pointed, 'Is that pubic hair?'

Looking down to where she was pointing, I saw several black hairs 'down there'.

'I think so. I'm not really sure though,' I mumbled, my cheeks burning red. I was ten years old and didn't really know what she was talking about.

She pushed the towel aside to get a better look.

'Those are definitely pubic hairs. Why didn't you tell me?'

Feeling awkward, I pulled away from Mom.

'I didn't even know they were there, sorry.'

She started to say something else, but I wasn't paying attention. I was too busy trying to make the towel cover my body up. *Why don't I want to be naked around Mom anymore?* I felt uneasy.

She was still talking when I got up to go downstairs. I moved carefully so as not to expose myself. I tore through the clothes in the laundry room until I finally found a pair of shorts and a T-shirt that wasn't dirty, and put them on. I felt relieved and weirdly safe, now that I was covered. I went back upstairs to help Mom with the Sudoku puzzle.

I sat back down on the arm of the couch. Mom stopped playing, turned and stared at me.

'Why are you wearing clothes?' she asked, confused.

Not wanting to upset her, I tried to calm her, 'I don't know. I just feel better wearing clothes now. It's not a big deal.'

Her anger ignited. I could see it in her eyes and I felt afraid again.

'Well, I know it's not a big deal, but you've never had a problem with it before, so why all of a sudden? Did I make you uncomfortable asking about your pubic hair?' she asked defensively.

'Kind of. I just want to be covered from now on,' I said staring at the floor.

She shook her head and returned to Sudoku. She couldn't let it go though.

'You don't have to hide things from me,' she went on. There was something menacing about the way she said that.

After a few minutes of awkward silence, she changed the subject.

'You need to go to bed in half an hour. School starts next week and you need to start getting back into a sleep schedule.'

'I know. I can't wait to go back to school,' I said, perking up, happily kicking my legs. School was my escape.

I did what I was told and went up to our bedroom. Out of habit, I stopped outside the door, and took my clothes off ready for bed. I was pulling my shirt over my head when I had a revelation. *If I don't like being naked around my mom, then why am I about to sleep naked with her?* I yanked the shirt back over my head and pulled my shorts up.

I crawled into the bed, covering myself with the blanket. *I think I'm going to start sleeping in my own room soon*, I thought as I drifted off to sleep.

• • •

I chose the following night to break the news to Mom. The day after that was going to be my first day of my final year at elementary school, and I wanted to be more grown up. I wasn't afraid of sleeping alone anymore. I was used to the mice and the rats and the creaky noises in the basement. I wasn't scared about the ghosts from the murders anymore. I was less scared about the world since I'd tried to kill myself. It was like something inside me had died already.

I nervously played with my blouse as I rolled the words around on my tongue.

'I'm going to sleep in my own bed from now on,' I blurted out.

A big smile appeared on Mom's face.

'That's wonderful!' she exclaimed.

I wasn't expecting that. *Why is Mom so against me wearing my clothes, but happy for me to sleep in my own bed?* I had lost count of how many times she had turned from nasty to nice.

'But just remember, you can sleep with me if you get scared. I don't have any sheets for your bed, but we can get some tomorrow after school. You can sleep on just the mattress for tonight. Now, let's get your bed ready.'

I grabbed my pillows while Mom grabbed my blankets and we went into my room. It looked more like a museum of my artefacts than a bedroom. There were cobwebs everywhere, because nobody had been in there to swat them down. I had an empty bookshelf on the far wall, a desk keeping the closet door shut, a dresser filled with books and my bed. The air smelt stale and unlived in. But there wasn't much trash in here, just in the doorway. The room didn't have a door, so the rubbish had spilled in from the hallway.

'Now, we're going to have to get you an alarm clock, and sheets, and decorations. Is there anything you want?' she asked, tossing my blankets on the bed before splodging on the end of it.

I scrunched up my nose in disgust. *That's gross, you're sitting naked on my bed.*

'Um, no. I think that will be good,' I said, arranging my pillows.

She patted my head and said, 'Well, kiddo, I'm proud of you. I'll wake you up in the morning.'

I turned off the light and crawled into my bed. It was much smaller than the bed I shared with my mom, but at least it wasn't soaked in pee, and there wasn't a sea of garbage to wade through to get there. The mattress was scratchy on my skin; I couldn't wait to get sheets.

It was hard to fall asleep. I was used to scrunching up in the corner to avoid Mom's pee leaking on me. I was also very excited because the first day of school was just hours away. I uncoiled myself into a starfish shape and I finally drifted off.

I was woken by Mom gently stroking my face.

'Good morning kiddo. Are you ready for school?' she asked smiling.

She was still being nice! It was unusual for her happy mood to last two days in a row.

I rubbed the sleep out of my eyes. Yawning, I nodded my head. I swung my legs off the bed, and noticed a few red bumps on my calves. I lifted my legs up for a better look – they were covered in dozens of red bumps.

'Mom, what are these?' I said, scratching them – they were really itchy.

As she inspected my legs, the rest of my body started to itch. I found a lot more of the same bumps on my arms. Under my shirt there were several more angry red bumps.

'You need to get out of those clothes and into the shower, right now,' she ordered, pushing me to the bathroom. 'There must be some sort of bug infestation in your mattress. We'll get you a new one this weekend.'

The bumps were everywhere – on my fingers, in between my toes, on my neck, and covering my arms and legs. It was my first day back at school and I looked like a freak. I'd gone from happy to sad in a matter of minutes. I buried my face in my hands.

I heard Mom gathering things throughout the house, her clothes being put on, her keys jingling. She came to the bathroom and said, 'I'm going to go to the store really quick and get you medicine and cream. Just keep getting ready for school.'

'I still have to go to school?' I whimpered while lathering my hair.

'Of course you are. You're not missing the first day,' she said, walking away.

I heard the door slam, just as I was rinsing the last bit of shampoo out of my hair. Even though I was done, I let the warm water run over my body. It made the bumps less itchy.

I dried off and put on the outfit I had laid out the night before. *Eww, my arms and legs look gross. I can't wear this*, I thought, inspecting the angry lumps.

I ran downstairs and started desperately searching for something else to wear. I dug through the pile of laundry, but only found one long sleeve shirt, and it was a nerdy science shirt. *I can't wear this on the first day, I'll get made fun of*. I tossed it on the dryer. I paused for a moment and scratched ferociously. I continued my search until Mom walked in the door, startling me.

'What are you doing?' she asked.

Still digging through the laundry, I explained, 'I can't wear my blouse to school. You can see all of the bumps. I have to find something nice because it's the first day.'

'You're right, but first you need to take some of this medicine,' she said, kneeling next to me. 'This will help with the itching.'

She handed me two little pink and white pills and an orange juice to wash them down. I popped them in my mouth and took a big glug. She then handed me two pain killers. I swallowed those too, and continued my search for a cute outfit.

Placing a hand on my shoulder, she said, 'Kiddo, stop. I've got some anti-itch lotion too. I need to dab it on. When we're done, I'll help you look for an outfit.'

I squirmed with each dab. The lotion was cold and slimy. Mom pulled my T-shirt down and patted me on the head.

'Okay kiddo, we're done.'

I spotted a pair of trousers that may have been

clean. I climbed over a pile of clothes and yanked them out from in between the dryer and the wall. I buried my nose in the trousers and took a big whiff. They didn't smell musty. *Perfect!* I thought, kicking my shorts off and sliding them on.

'I only need a shirt now,' I started foraging again.

'Here's a long sleeve shirt,' she said, holding up the nerdy yellow one I'd seen earlier.

Shaking my head, I said, 'I can't wear that. I'll be teased.'

'Well, what if you put this over it?' She held up a green, wide strapped tank top.

'Let me see how it looks.'

I grabbed it with one hand, and itched my belly with the other. Putting the two tops on, it actually looked good.

'I'll wear it. Thanks Mom,' I said. I sat on the stairs to put my shoes on.

I couldn't stop itching while in the car.

'Britney, stop that. You'll leave scars,' she barked.

'So you don't get too itchy at school, I'm going to give you four of the pink and white pills. Take them on your first and third break.'

She paused for a moment, chewing over the next part.

'Don't let anyone see you take them though, you could get in trouble,' she warned.

'Why would I get in trouble?' I asked, itching my arms furiously.

Rolling her eyes, she said, 'The school thinks any kid with pills is going to pass them out like candy. It's to protect other students. We don't need any suspicions being raised, so just take the pills discreetly.'

As we pulled up to the school, I was still itching. Instead of going to the usual drop-off location, Mom parked the car.

'I going to dab the anti-itch cream on you again. This has medicine in it too, so you can't show this to teachers,' she warned, holding up the tube.

It was a very warm morning, and I was sweating in all the layers I was wearing. Mom dabbed as many bug bites as she could with the cream, before the bell rang.

'I have to go, that means we have two minutes to get to class,' I panicked, pulling my tops down.

Mom looked around to check who was listening before leaning in.

'Okay, remember to take those pills at the first and third break time, and don't get caught. Love ya kiddo,' she whispered.

'Love you too Mom,' I said, grabbing my backpack and racing off. It was weird, when my mom was being nice to me it was like nothing else mattered.

•••

In class, I used the back of my chair to itch my back but that barely brought relief. I couldn't listen, I couldn't concentrate – my eyes were glued to the clock as I counted down the seconds before I could take the pink and white pills again. Finally, the bell rang. I grabbed my backpack and sprinted to the bathroom. I gobbled my pills and applied the itch cream. I couldn't get the bites on my back though and they were driving me crazy.

I had a bit of break time left and went out into the sunshine. All of my classmates were wearing shorts and short sleeve shirts. They were running around having fun. I was wearing heavy denim trousers, a shirt and a jumper. The heat was making my bumps itch even more. I sat alone on the steps, wiping the sweat from my forehead.

A lunch lady spotted me and came over.

'Why are you all bundled up like that? It's 80 degrees out,' she asked.

'It's not really a big deal. It's just what I wanted to

wear for the first day of school,' I lied, scratching at my arms and belly.

'Are you okay?' she asked, gently taking my arm and pushing up my sleeve.

'Yeah, I've just got a couple of bug bites.' I recoiled my arm with embarrassment.

'Taking off that long sleeve shirt will really help with the itching. Your sweat is on them, making them itch more. Let's go inside so you can take it off,' she said kindly.

She stood and held out her hand for me. I grabbed it, and followed her inside. She brought me to the teachers' bathroom, so I could change in privacy.

I took off my shirt and put my tank top back on. I hated what I saw in the mirror. I looked like a fat clown. My trousers were too short and my chubby stomach oozed out of the top of them. The tank top was also too short and looked like it had been shrunk in the wash. My arms had angry red bumps and scratches up and down them. Some of them were bleeding because I had scratched them too much.

I emerged from the bathroom with folded arms as I tried to cover my bites and rounded stomach. I was expecting to see my dinner lady, but my teacher and the head teacher were also waiting for me outside.

'Oh my goodness, Britney, are you okay?' my head teacher yelped, putting her hand over her mouth.

'I'm fine, it's just a few bug bites,' I said, defensively.

'Well, we're going to call your mom. You need lighter clothes to wear because it's hot. I'm also concerned about the bug bites. Is that all of them on your arms there?' she asked, squatting so she was eye level with me.

I burst into tears.

'No. I stopped counting at 100 bites,' I lifted my tank top a few inches.

They all let out a gasp.

My teacher grabbed my hand and led me into the head's office. She left me alone with the head teacher and I started blubbering again. I watched helplessly as the head dialled my mom's work number. *Mom's going to be mad at me for not keeping our secret.*

• • •

'Britney? Britney?' repeated my head teacher, waving her hand to get my attention.

'What's happening?' I mumbled; I was in a daze.

'Your mom will be here shortly to pick you up. We want you to feel better. Do you want to sit in the teachers' lounge and have a snack while you wait?' she asked, rummaging through her drawer.

'Yes, that sounds good,' I sniffled.

She grabbed a small paper bag from the drawer and took my hand.

'Come with me, we'll get you set up,' she said reassuringly.

The door swung open and there was a big red couch with a TV in front of it. I looked at my head teacher and she nodded with approval. I skipped over to the couch and plopped myself down. I grabbed the remote and surfed the channels until I found some cartoons to watch. She handed me a paper bag. *What's this?* I peered inside.

'There's a few snacks in there for you. What would you like to drink? We've got milk, strawberry and chocolate, or apple juice?'

'Can I have the strawberry milk?' I replied excitedly.

Nodding her head, she disappeared out of the room.

I rummaged through the bag of snacks she had left. There was a Snickers bar, a bag of pretzels and an orange. I ripped the Snickers open, savouring every bite.

Only a few minutes had passed when Mom and the head teacher came into the room.

'Hi Mom,' I said, in between bites.

'Hi kiddo. You feeling any better?' she asked, sounding out of steam.

'Eh, kind of. I'm still really itchy though,' I scratched my arm.

'We're sorry to call you out here in the middle of the day, but she was too over-dressed for the weather, and then we saw the bug bites. She looked miserable; we want her to feel better,' my head told my mom.

Mom sat next to me and rummaged through her handbag. 'I understand, I just didn't want her missing the first day. She must have brought bedbugs back from camp or something. Boy, do they sure have good timing.'

She pulled out a bottle and handed me two of the pink and white pills.

'Here, take these.' She passed me some milk.

As soon as I had gulped them down Mom grabbed my hand.

'Thank you for taking care of her,' she said, pulling me along.

'Not a problem. Just keep us informed. We can't wait to have her back,' the head said, waving us good bye. She must have bought the story about summer camp.

As Mom started the car, I started to tremble. I

was waiting for her to explode with anger.

But she turned to me and apologised, 'Hon, I'm sorry. I didn't mean to put you through that.'

'It's fine Mom. I wanted to go to school today,' I said, relieved she was still being nice. I buckled up.

The rest of the car ride was silent, except for the crunching noise of the pretzels as I ate them. When we pulled into the driveway, Mom surprised me.

'I took the rest of the day off. We need to get your bed out of the house.'

'Great, but where are we going to put it?' I asked.

Sighing deeply, she said, 'I haven't thought of that yet.'

• • •

I changed into a pair of shorts and my legs felt a hundred times better for breathing. Because Mom left work early she didn't have a chance to grab food so we made macaroni. We rarely had home-cooked food, and even then it came from a box.

Then we got to work. We had to clear a path from my room to the garage door, moving all of the crap from the edge of the stairs to prevent it from avalanching down.

'Let me worry about the mattress. Just stay out of the way.'

She grabbed the foot of my mattress. Giving it a

good yank, Mom lost her grip, and fell back against the wall.

'That is a lot heavier than I was expecting,' she spluttered.

She tried again, this time grabbing the handles on the edge. Mom braced herself, heaved, but toppled down again, with a loud thud. One of the handles broke.

'God damn it!' she yelled. 'Britney, help me push this thing outside. Get in the front, and guide it, I'll push from the back.' She ushered me past her.

I shuddered, thinking about the bedbugs. But I also really wanted that mattress gone.

It took forever to get it to the upstairs door. There were so many corners that we had to shove it around. It didn't help that the mattress weighed a million pounds. Even though we had cleared a path to the door, trash and clothes were dragged along with us.

We pushed the mattress down to the basement. It slid all the way, landing with a loud thud, the springs inside, humming. I opened the door, and yanked, and yanked, trying to coax it out of the door. My mom gave it a nudge. Finally, it was on the porch.

'Now what?' I asked, panting.

'I've been thinking, and we're going to throw it

in the pit,' she spluttered, in between breaths. 'You ready?' she asked.

I positioned myself at the front of the mattress. As we dragged it across the porch, it kept catching on wood. Every few feet, we were jolted to a halt. Our back yard was huge, and Mom didn't like mowing the grass – it came up to my knees like a jungle. It was impossible to walk to the pool, let alone drag a heavy mattress there. But we finally got to the edge of the pit and tossed the bug-ridden mattress in.

I nervously looked around the back yard for prying eyes, thankful that we didn't have any neighbours. We were also pretty secluded from traffic, the lilac bushes lined the back yard, and none of the drivers passing could see what we were doing. The closest house was next to the liquor store across the junction from our house, and it was abandoned most of the time.

'Um Mom, what am I going to sleep on now?' I asked, looking at my mattress.

'What about that chair? You know, the one that folds out into a bed?' she said, walking back towards the house.

'Yeah, that'll work. I'll set it up later. So how long am I going to be out of school?' I asked.

'Just a few days, until the bumps clear up.'

'I'm getting a new bed this weekend, aren't I?' I asked nervously.

No reply.

Oh God, please buy me a new bed so I don't have to sleep in the piss stains again.

Later on that evening, I carried the fold-out bed into my bedroom and set it up on the box spring base. It was green, made up of four foam sections, and was much smaller than the old mattress.

'Mom, the fold-out bed is nowhere near as big as the box spring,' I shouted.

'It'll be fine,' she yelled back.

I slept on that tiny fold-out bed for six months, until a mattress store was having a sale.

CHAPTER 8

I was very excited to be starting middle school. The last year at elementary had been difficult. I did my best to fit in, but sensed that my friends thought I was weird. I wasn't allowed to have them over to play, and I wasn't up to date on any of the latest trends in music, games or clothes. I didn't have many friends so this was my chance to finally make some. My excitement turned to nerves as I panicked over whether anyone would like me.

The bus pulled into the drop off area, and all of the middle schoolers piled out. I followed the other kids to the sixth-grade wing and found my locker. I hung up my backpack and grabbed my stack of books for my first class. I still had twenty minutes before class started.

I didn't want to look like a nerd by being early, so I walked around looking for friends from elementary school. Finally, I recognised a girl, standing in a group.

119

'Hey Sara, what's up?' I said, smiling.

'Oh, hey Britney. Nothing,' she said, turning her back on me.

I tried again. I weaved myself into the group.

'Hi everyone, I'm Britney,' I announced.

A few of the kids started giggling.

'Oh, what did I just miss?' I asked innocently.

'Nothing, weirdo. We don't want you around and you can't take the hint,' hissed a blonde girl.

I felt the heat burning in my cheeks. I looked to the floor and scurried away like a beaten dog. *Just go to class and try and make friends with those kids*, I consoled myself.

There were three people waiting for class to start as I walked in.

'Hi, I'm Britney,' I said, taking a seat next to a girl in the middle of the room.

She rolled her eyes with irritation.

'What elementary school did you go to?' I asked, desperately trying to keep the conversation going.

She got up and snatched her backpack.

'Look, it doesn't matter. I don't want to talk to you,' she scowled, moving to a different chair. The two other kids in the class sniggered.

The clock said there was eight minutes left until class started. Embarrassed, I took out a pencil and a notebook, to look busy. *What the heck is going on? Why doesn't anyone want to talk to me?* I thought, while doodling.

The bell rang and the kids filed in the door. Someone sat next to the girl who ignored me, and they talked and laughed like they were best friends. Everyone had someone to chat to, to catch up on the summer. Everyone except me. No one wanted to sit next to me, and I didn't want to look desperate changing chairs.

The teacher walked in as the final bell rang. I'd never been so happy to see a teacher.

'Okay class. We are just waiting for the students who can't find their class,' he said, slurping his coffee. The students continued their conversations while we waited.

The only seats left were the two next to me, so when the last two students arrived, my eyes lit up. Friends at last! The boy, who was quite chubby, plopped down in the seat to the right of me. But the girl moved her seat as far away from me as she could get. *I didn't smell anymore, did I?* I subtly tried to sniff the armpit of my top. It smelt of my lilac flower deodorant to my relief. *So what am I doing wrong?*

I was sure the other kids had a different reason to be mean to me. Everyone was walking around with the new MP3 players, branded clothes, cool accessories and all of the girls got to wear make-up. I had a CD player that was so broken it shouldn't still have be working, all of my clothes came from second-hand stores, and I was only allowed to wear lip gloss. I wasn't allowed to have a TV in my room or even a radio. The only radio I got to listen to was in the car, and that was my mom's 1980s rock.

'All right, everyone up and go to the back of the class,' our teacher said, clapping his hands enthusiastically.

Chairs screeched across the floor, and everyone let out a groan as they got up and shuffled to the back of the class. The teacher started reading out names, one by one, pointing to the seat they were assigned to. The girls squealed with delight if they were sat next to a friend. The guys high-fived each other as they took their seats. Halfway through the list, my name was called. I was sat in between two girls who were friends. Instead of talking to me, they talked through me. I may as well have been invisible.

The same thing happened in every class. I wouldn't know anyone, or the kids I did know didn't want to know me. Anyone I introduced myself to, turned cold, or didn't even respond. Lunch break finally rolled around and I got into the lunch queue.

The selection was massive and I didn't know where to start. There were sandwiches, hamburgers, hot dogs and pizzas. To the right were the specialties for the day. In the middle of the room there was an island with the salad bar, where the drinks and snacks were also located. Overwhelmed, I grabbed a stuffed crust pizza, salad, chips and a chocolate milk.

Once I had paid, I scanned the lunch room for a place to sit. The cliques were so obvious. Everyone was divided by race, and within that there were sub groups – the popular kids, the nerdy kids, the gothic kids, the athletic kids. I had no idea where I fitted in. I finally found a girl who I recognised from a few of my classes. Clasping my tray, I walked up to her table, and said:

'Hi, it's Claire, right? I'm Britney, we have a few classes with each other. Can I sit down?'

Smiling, she pulled the chair out for me.

'Yeah, sit down. We've got English and math together.'

Claire introduced me to everyone at the table. They were all friendly, and the lunch period seemed to pass really fast.

'Will you guys be sitting around here tomorrow?' I asked nervously. I didn't want to sound needy or desperate, although that was the way I was feeling.

'For sure. We'll keep a chair open for you,' said Claire, as we left the cafeteria.

Finally, I had found a friend.

• • •

I made a few more friends over the next month. I was teased every once in a while for my weight, but it wasn't so bad now I had found some girls who liked me. In gym class one day we played dodge ball. I started getting into it, and it helped me come out of my shell even more. For the first time, I felt like I was good at something.

I'd caught someone out in a game and I did my first celebration dance. I was so proud, my arms and legs just took over. I jumped into the air, reaching my hands to the sky. A rush of adrenaline pulsed through me and I realised what it felt like to be happy.

That lunch, I got my usual, stuffed crust pizza, a salad, an orange and a skim milk. I walked up to Claire's table with a big smile on my face. As I was putting my tray on the table, Claire placed her books on the empty seat.

'You can't sit with us anymore,' she said, crossing her arms.

I laughed it off, thinking it was a joke. I moved her books onto the table.

'No, I'm serious. You can't eat with us anymore,' she said, rudely. Her friends at the table wouldn't look at me. They awkwardly pushed their food around their plates, or stared into the distance.

'But why? What did I do?' I whimpered, picking up my tray.

'You were way too competitive in gym class. You enjoyed hitting people with the dodge balls,' she said, in a condescending voice.

'You're kidding me?' I was mad at her reasoning. 'That's what we were supposed to do.'

She turned away, with her nose high in the air. I left the table as my face turned red with embarrassment and sadness. I threw away my untouched food and headed straight to the bathroom. I slammed the stall, and sat on the toilet, crying. *I could barely make friends at the beginning of the year. What am I going to do now?* I buried my face in my hands.

The bell rang and I had to wipe the tears away from my eyes. I blew my nose and went to my next class. The next couple of days I didn't know where to eat my lunch. I drifted from table to table, asking if they had a seat free for me.

Some kids were just downright mean. They said horrible things like, 'You're not cool enough to sit with us' or 'You're so fat, you'd take up two spots'.

Some of the girls would smile at me but they still wouldn't let me sit with them, and some of the girls were so nasty, they even taunted me about my dad. They called me 'the child of a whore'. How did they know? That high at the dodge ball game was so fleeting I couldn't even remember it anymore.

• • •

For weeks, I ate lunch alone, on a bench in the hallway. Kids would pass by and laugh at me. 'Wow, what a loser,' they would joke; not caring that I could hear them. Every comment cut deep like a knife.

Every night I cried in bed. I wished I was born someone different.

'Mom, why don't the kids at school like me? The girls I went to elementary with won't even be my friends anymore.'

She couldn't be bothered to look away from the computer as she answered.

'I don't know. Maybe you're weird. Or, you might have to try harder,' she shrugged.

I fell silent and stared at the trash. *Everyone hates me. I'm just like the trash.*

I couldn't take the rejection and the name calling anymore. I shut down and stopped trying. It was easier to blend into the background, and have no friends, than it was to meet new people.

After another lonely lunch, I headed to science. The room was set up differently. Instead of rows of desks, they were clumped into groups of four. I sat next to Brooke and Maggie, who talked to me in class but ignored me at lunch or in the hallway.

'Hey Britney, what's up?' Brooke asked, as I was rummaging through my backpack.

When Brooke or Maggie asked me a question like that, they didn't really care. When they first started talking to me, I thought they had a real interest in becoming my friends. After a while though, I realised they talked to me because I got good grades, and if we worked in a group, I would do all the work. I didn't care though. It meant I had some girls to talk to.

Mike, Brooke's 'boyfriend', was the fourth on our table. I didn't think they were actually boyfriend and girlfriend because they didn't kiss, or even hold hands, but it was how they told it. I'd never had a boyfriend. I couldn't even make friends, let alone have a boyfriend. I was an ugly freak.

The final bell rang and everyone went silent. The teacher started writing on the blackboard.

'We're going to be doing a group project, in groups of four,' he said scribbling across the board.

Mike, Brooke and Maggie high-fived each other while I sat there quietly. *They're excited because they can ride on my coat tails and get an A without having to do anything.*

'Okay, I'm picking groups this time,' he faced the class.

He picked up a sheet of paper and walked over to the group of desks nearest to him.

'Brooke, Travis, Sara, Deckard. You're in this group,' he said, pointing to the cluster of desks.

Brooke let out a disheartened sigh. She grabbed her bag and shuffled to the front of the class. I was excited. *Maybe I'll do an equal share of the work instead of all of it*, I thought, packing up my backpack.

'Britney, Nancy, Zach, Troy. You four are there,' said my teacher, pointing to a cluster in the corner.

This'll be fun. I know Troy from elementary. Maybe I can get to know Nancy and Zach.

I said 'Hi' to Troy, and introduced myself to Zach. Nancy appeared mad at the world, and didn't seem to care.

'Hi, I'm Britney,' I said to the girl, sticking my hand out for a greeting.

'Yep, Nancy,' she said abruptly, quickly shaking my hand before sinking heavily into the chair and staring sullenly into the distance. She was about the same size as I was – chubby. Her skin had a slight shade of chocolate, and her hair was beautiful –

perfect little ringlets of black hair, which stopped just at her jaw line. She wore black jeans with holes in the knees, and braces, which hung loose by her knees, not over her shoulders. Her big black hoodie had safety pins all over it. Some of the pins made shapes, like stars and broken hearts.

Our teacher hushed the class, and explained the project. We had to make a terrarium – a garden in a plastic soda bottle. The team with the most diverse terrarium would get an A. Because we had to grow plants and sustain life, the project was going to last three months.

I was relieved that my other teammates also wanted to do the work. It wasn't going to be left up to me.

The next day at lunch, instead of eating at the bench in the hallway I looked for Nancy. For some reason, I really wanted to be her friend, even though she had been rude. I searched the lunchroom for her black hoodie, hoping she was wearing it. After a few minutes of weaving between the tables, I found her.

She was sitting at a table in the corner with kids who were also dressed in black. I'd seen some of those kids being bullied for being a goth. I'd been bullied too so that was okay by me. I took a deep breath and walked over.

'Hey Nancy. Can I sit with you?' I asked, trying to sound confident.

Looking me up and down, she nodded her head, and pointed to the spot next to her. I sat down and started eating. I tried to include myself in their conversation, but they were talking about manga and anime. I had no idea what any of that stuff was. Fed up of not knowing what they were so excited about, I asked, 'What's manga?'

Nancy let out an excited squeal, and said, 'OMG! Manga is a graphic novel from Japan.'

It seemed like everyone started digging through their backpacks at the same time. All of a sudden I had six different books thrown in front of me. Nancy laid them out, and started explaining each book in detail. When she was finished, she tossed two books in front of me.

'Here, take these to read. I'm done with them anyway. It won't take long to read them, you can give them back to me tomorrow at lunch,' she said, taking a bite of mashed potato.

'Wow, thanks. You guys are really cool,' I said, flipping through the books.

A boy sitting across from me, butted in, 'Yeah, but nobody else really thinks so.'

I spent my lunch laughing, and I was really

enjoying myself. When break was over, Nancy and I walked to science class together, joined to each other by headphones. She wanted me to listen to some music from Japan called J-pop. I couldn't understand what they were saying, but the music was fun and engaging. We kept getting into trouble in class because we wouldn't stop talking.

After school, I was going to walk to the hospital where Mom worked. It was about a two mile walk and I hadn't even made it past the soccer fields when I heard someone yelling my name from a distance. Confused, I turned around, searching for whoever it was. It was Nancy, she was running towards me, yelling my name. I stopped and waited for her to catch up with me.

'I saw you walking, and I live in this direction. Want company?' she huffed and puffed.

'Yeah sure,' I said, excited that she had gone out of her way to catch up with me.

We started walking again, and Nancy grabbed my arm.

'Have you seen the nature reserve?' she asked, pulling me onto the soccer fields.

'Nature reserve? No,' I said, stumbling. I had a habit of being clumsy.

She flashed me a cheeky look and led me into the

woods just behind the sports pitches. We walked across a small wooden bridge over a creek and emerged into an opening in the woods. There were makeshift benches made out of large flat boulders and tree trunks.

'Not here,' she beckoned me onwards.

Nancy led the way through a maze of dusty paths. We vaulted over fallen trees, and ducked below low branches. Without her, I would have got completely lost. We pushed through some bushes, and out of nowhere, we were back on a city street.

'I like going home this way. It's so pretty,' Nancy broke the silence.

'I didn't even know that was there. Thanks for taking me through it,' I said, smiling.

She started walking, but I suddenly stopped. *Where was I?* I didn't even know which street we were on. Before I'd started school here, I'd never needed to come to this part of town. I felt a little scared.

Nancy realised I wasn't following her. 'What's wrong?'

'I don't really know where I'm at. I need to get to the hospital, it's where my mom works,' I admitted, a little embarrassed.

Chuckling, she waved me over to her, and we kept walking. Over her shoulder she said, 'Follow me, it's in the same direction as my house.'

During our walk, we talked more about anime and manga. She gave me one of her earphones and we listened to more J-pop. We finally got to an area that I recognised, only minutes from the hospital. Nancy turned off the music and pulled the earphone out of my ear.

'My house is a block down there,' she said, pointing down the road. 'Wanna see my house?' she asked, putting her MP3 player away.

Looking down the road in the direction of the hospital, I nervously said, 'Sure, but could I use your phone to call my mom? She'll get worried about me.'

Nancy nodded her head, and we started down the road. When we got to her house, I was right on Nancy's heel. I was about to follow her inside, when she stopped, and looked at me nervously.

'Um, could you wait here for a second? I have to make sure my parents aren't home,' she said, nervously.

'Sure. Why?' I asked, confused.

'I'll explain in a second. Just let me check first.' she said, disappearing into her house.

After a few minutes, Nancy re-emerged through her front door, and she quickly ushered me in. Before she closed the door, she looked up and down the street. She then locked the door behind us, and began to apologise.

'I'm sorry. My mom and dad don't like me having friends over. I just had to make sure they weren't here or on their way. The phone is up there,' she said, pointing to the kitchen, up a few stairs.

I was too busy staring at how clean Nancy's house was. Everything had its place – it was like one of those show homes. The couches were cream without a single stain. The cushions had been plumped up and neatly arranged. My eyes were drawn to the coffee table where there was a vase filled with beautiful lilac flowers. I'd never seen flowers as decoration before. Nothing in my house was there to make it look pretty and homely. I gently stroked the purple petals and a feeling of sadness washed over me.

I reluctantly walked over to the phone and dialled my mom.

Nancy started running around her house. It seemed like she was doing chores, sweeping up the kitchen and dining room, and throwing clothes by the washing machine.

'Hello, food service. How may I help you?' Mom said. Her politeness sounded forced.

'Hey Mom. It's me. I just wanted to call and let you know I might be a few minutes late. I made a friend today, and her house is on the way to the hospital. I'm here now,' I said, dancing around Nancy's broom.

Nancy whispered in my ear.

'Ask her if you can hang out with me. It's video game night at the library. I just have to finish up my chores. It'll take me fifteen minutes.'

Interrupting whatever my mom was saying, I said, 'Hey Mom. Nancy, my new friend, wants me to hang out with her. There is something going on at the library she wants to take me to. Can I go?'

I think Mom was left speechless for a moment as she realised I did have a friend.

'Um, uh, uh. Can you swing by the hospital first?' she stuttered. 'You know, drop your backpack off. I'd also like to meet her, and I'll have snacks for you guys.'

I covered the phone with my hand. 'Can we go to the hospital first? My mom wants me to drop off my backpack, and she wants to meet you. Oh, and she'll have snacks for us; she's a cook.' I looked up at Nancy.

Smiling she said, 'I love snacks!'

'Thank you Mom. We'll be there in a while. We still have about half a mile to walk, and Nancy has to finish up her chores,' I explained. I was excited.

'Okay kiddo. Be safe while walking. Bye.'

Nancy poured me a glass of punch and pulled a chair out at the dining table. It was weird sitting at a table in someone's home, but it felt good. I checked the glass to see if it was clean, a default reaction.

'It's clean,' Nancy laughed. She gave me a strange look.

'Oh yeah, I know, I was just checking out the design,' I lied.

Nancy had disappeared upstairs to finish her chores when I heard the garage door opening. She quickly ran back down, grabbed my backpack and my hand, and dragged me through the house to her front door.

'You have to leave now. Just wait outside, I'm almost done,' she whispered urgently.

I was confused.

'Why, what's going on?' I panicked.

'Remember, I told you. My parents don't like it when I bring friends over. I'll get into a lot of trouble if they find out you've been inside. Now go.' She nudged me out of the front door.

Just as I was stepping out, I heard what I assumed to be her father, announcing his arrival home.

'Wait here. I'll be just a sec,' she whispered, shutting the door on me.

After a few minutes, Nancy appeared around the side of the house. 'I'm so sorry about that,' she said.

'That's okay. I'm not allowed to have friends over either,' I said, as we started walking.

'Your parents are weird too?' she giggled.

Maybe the reason my mom doesn't want me having friends over is because she doesn't want anyone seeing the trash, I thought to myself. It was a light bulb moment.

'Something like that,' I said lightly. I played it down. If only she knew the truth.

As we made our way to the hospital, the idea that Mom knew what she was doing to us and wanted to hide her secret from the world swirled around in my head.

I left Nancy in the cafeteria while I dropped off my backpack with Mom in the kitchen. She returned with me to where Nancy was waiting.

'Hi, I'm Gene. Britney's mom. I've got to grab your snacks. Feel free to have some drinks,' Mom said.

My mom can seem so normal when she is out of our house. When she is wearing clothes. She can be so nice too.

Nasty, nice, nasty, nice – you never knew what you were going to get from her, and I was left riding her emotional swing. At least she was being nice to my new friend.

Mom returned with a brown paper bag filled to the brim. She put it down on the counter, peeling it open to reveal the goodies inside. There were oatmeal chocolate chip cookies, multi-layer cookie bars, chocolate dipped treats and pretzels.

'You two are the first to try this batch of cookies. They should be delicious,' she said, proud of her creation. 'So what's going on at the library tonight?'

'Well, today is the video game competition,' Nancy grinned.

'Wow, that's amazing. I didn't know the library did that sort of stuff.' Mom was somewhat taken aback.

'Yeah, a few years ago the library thought it would be better to have us kids do fun things like this every other week, instead of getting in trouble when we're bored,' Nancy said, munching on a pretzel.

'Very cool. Well, I have to get back to work. Have fun, I'll pick you up after work,' Mom said, walking back towards the kitchen.

Nancy and I left for the library. Our eyes locked and Nancy flashed me the biggest grin. I knew at that moment, that we were going to be friends for a long time. We both were trying to run away from where we came from.

• • •

Nancy and I were inseparable after that. But if we wanted to hang out, we had to find somewhere to go and something to do. I couldn't go to her house because her parents were very strict, and she would get in trouble. I couldn't have her stay at my house, because of all of the trash – not that she knew that was the reason. Sometimes, if the weather turned bad, it was annoying that we didn't have a home we could just hang out in and ended up at the library, but the upsides far outweighed the bad.

Days that Nancy was busy with her band, I started getting into some after-school activities. I joined kung fu and the tennis team, trying to get away from the house and also hoping to lose some weight, to fit in with more kids from school. I discovered both sports came naturally to me, and I loved participating. Nancy encouraged me to come out of my shell, and that's just what I did.

I only had to spend a couple of evenings at home a week now. The rest of the time, I would get back just before bed. I'd go straight to my room and avoid as much of the trash as I could. Once I closed my eyes I could imagine I was somewhere else as I drifted off to sleep.

Thanks to Nancy, I had a whole new life. She didn't know it, but she had become my saviour from that hellhole.

CHAPTER 9

'I'm going to miss you so much! And I'm super jealous. You get to miss the last two weeks of school.' Nancy said after school, giving me a hug.

'I know, I'm going to miss you too. I'm kind of sad I won't be there for the last two weeks. I'm going to miss all of our pizza parties,' I said, laughing.

'But you're going to be in China. There is no way you can be sad. You are sooo lucky,' she said, throwing her hands into the air.

My mom honked the car horn twice, and waved at me, impatiently. Rolling my eyes, I said, 'I have to go. I'll see you when I get back. Bye.'

I jumped in the front seat and shut the door.

'Sorry to rush you kiddo, but we have to say bye to your grandma and we have a four hour car ride. I want to go before it gets too dark,' Mom explained.

At my grandma's house, she had a surprise going away dinner waiting for us. She had come to most of the kung fu demonstrations I'd participated in, and was really proud that I was training in another country. Aunt Maxine and Louise stopped to wish me luck on the journey.

• • •

It was a long car ride, and an even longer plane ride to Los Angeles. It was my first trip abroad and I kept wiggling in my seat. I wanted to fast-forward time so I could be there already.

As we were waiting for our luggage, Mom smiled at me and said, 'I'm really glad you wanted me to come with you to kung fu camp.'

I shrugged my shoulders, and watched the luggage carousel. I was going to be twelve soon, and starting my second year of middle school. I wasn't a baby anymore and wished she wouldn't treat me like one.

'I wanted to have fun with you. You know, get out of the house,' I lied. I'd joined the kung fu club at school so I could spend even more evenings away from home – away from Mom. I could never find the strength to tell Mom what I really felt.

I spotted one of our suitcases – an ugly green tatty case with hundreds of coloured, tacky flowers embroidered on it. I ran over, and dragged it off the carousel. Looking across to Mom in the distance, my angry thoughts bubbled over. *The only reason*

*you're here is because you pushed and pushed to
come. I finally agreed, but what I really wanted was
to have a break from you and the house.*

We packed all of our luggage into the trunk of
a taxi, and headed to our hotel. We had arrived in
LA several days before the school's flight left for
China. It was cheaper for us to fly like this instead
of catching a connecting flight.

We dropped off our luggage in the hotel room
and started sightseeing. I saw a whole new side to
my mom. She was happy and smiling. She didn't
get angry over stupid stuff, and she was active and
wanted to spend time with me. Usually she would
just sit in front of the computer playing solitary
games until she went to bed. I started to feel glad
my mom was with me.

We ended up on the beach. It was my first time
touching the Pacific Ocean. I was up to my ankles in
the water when Mom yelled from the shore, 'Don't
go out any further. I don't need you getting bitten
by a shark.'

Hearing the word 'shark' scared the hell out of
me, and I ran to the shore.

It was getting dark, so we grabbed a pizza and
went back to the hotel. For the first time in my
life, I didn't have to worry about walking across a

garbage covered floor. The bathroom was clean, the floor wasn't wet with piss. Best of all, if my mom peed the bed, I wouldn't have to wash the blankets.

The next day we had to pack up and move to another hotel. In four days, we stayed in three different hotels. My mom was kind of cheap like that – she got a better deal if she changed hotels than if we stayed at the same one.

The day we left for China finally arrived. I met all of my kung fu friends at the airport. Many had their parents with them too, so I decided maybe it wasn't so bad having Mom along.

The flight was long, but I could hang out with my friends, so it was bearable. We watched movies and played card games. Upon landing, we met our translator, Jackie. Instead of going straight to the hotel, we went sightseeing in the Forbidden City and Tiananmen Square. The architecture was beautiful; I had never seen anything like it before.

After a few hours, we went to our hotel to drop off our luggage, and then met everyone at a restaurant around the corner. There was a stuffed sea turtle mounted on the wall in the entrance with fishing nets draped across it. We sat down, fifteen to a table, to eat a family style meal. I didn't know what I was eating, but it was good.

The Chinese in the restaurant made fun of us when we had to ask for forks instead of just using the chopsticks.

Back at the hotel, Mom and I dropped onto the bed from exhaustion. We had survived a sixteen hour flight, followed by sightseeing and dinner. Mom had got us a double bed to share, but I didn't mind so much because I wouldn't have to change the sheets if Mom had an accident in the night.

• • •

I woke up at 6 a.m., crazy excited for the day ahead. We were going to see the Great Wall. We didn't have to go until 9.30 a.m., but I couldn't wait. I patted the sheets beside me. Relief – they were dry, Mom had made it through the night. I woke her up and we went to breakfast in the lobby of the hotel. They had everything – Western food, Chinese food, omelette, fruit, desserts, it was more like brunch. I grabbed a big fruit plate. When I came back to the table, Mom was stuffing her face from a plate that had a giant pyramid of cakes, eggs, pancakes, ham and stir-fry on it. She looked disgusting – syrup dribbled down the front of her shirt as she smacked her lips together. At points, she was fisting food into her mouth.

I knew this good spell wouldn't last.

I did my best not to associate myself with her, and moved to eat with my friends. I sat with Meg, Robbie and Joey. We planned a sleepover in Meg's room for that night. We finished eating and waited outside for the tour bus to arrive.

On the bus we played card games, trying to pass the time. At one point, we had twenty of us playing with six decks. Our parents kept hushing us, and the bus driver yelled at us to be quiet, in Chinese. We didn't care though, we kept playing, squealing with excitement. It felt so good to have fun and not worry about my chores. I felt a million miles away from my problems, from the trash.

We spent half of the day walking the Great Wall of China. I felt so small compared to the rest of the wall, and so humbled, knowing I was standing where so many people had lost their lives. We then browsed the flea market in the parking lot. I picked up some postcards to send to Nancy and my grandparents.

At the end of the day we crowded in Meg's room. Her mom ordered pizza and we watched movies Meg had brought on the trip with her. She was smart, and had also brought a DVD player in case the hotel didn't have one. It was a really good thing Meg had planned ahead as there was only one TV channel broadcast in English, and all it played was old, black-and-white Westerns. We filled up our bellies on pizza, and passed out late into the night.

I went back to my room in the morning, still smiling from my fun night with my friends. I pushed open the door and my face dropped. The room was trashed. Clothes were strewn all around, there were half a dozen takeaway boxes from Mom's dinner the night before. The pizza boxes were open on the floor, stinking the room out. The worst smell though, was the acid pong of her pee. I walked in the rest of the way, and there she was – sleeping on her bed, naked. The blanket was in a heap on the floor, and there was a yellow pool under her.

'Mom, I'm back,' I said, shaking her leg.

She could barely open her eyes.

'Did you have fun?' she groaned in a tired voice.

'Yeah, we ate pizza and watched movies,' I said, picking up her clothes.

She pulled herself out of bed and headed for the bathroom. I could see pee running down her legs with each step, soaking into the carpet. When she got into the bathroom she didn't even close the door.

'Britney, come here,' she ordered.

Hesitantly, I walked over. She was sitting, naked, on the toilet.

'Yeah?' I cringed.

Her faced creased as she strained for a poop.

'Well, what kind of pizza did you eat? What movies did you watch?' she asked.

I walked away, I didn't want to see my mom go to the bathroom.

'We had peperoni and sausage pizza. They had some other weird toppings that you don't see in the States, but Meg's mom wouldn't let us get them,' I answered. 'And we watched a whole bunch of movies, but we didn't really pay attention because we were playing card games.'

She started talking about her night, but I wasn't listening. I was so mad that I had to deal with the same stuff that I had to cope with at home. *I'm not even in the same country*, I wanted to scream. I hoped my trip was going to be an escape from the mess and *her*, but she had just brought it all with her.

I started getting dressed for training as my mom came out of the bathroom. I was sitting on my bed, when she sat next to me, naked. *You have no courtesy, your legs are still wet from the pee that dripped out on your walk to the bathroom and you sit on my bed. Get off!* All of a sudden, she wrapped her big arm around my shoulders and pulled me in for a hug. I tried to push her away, but the only thing I could push on was her naked flabby body. I was disgusted, but I didn't know what to do.

'I was worried about you kiddo. I knew you were safe, but we are in a whole different country,' she said letting go of me.

She got up, leaving a huge wet patch on the blankets. It was like she didn't wipe after using the toilet. I shuddered, knowing that I was going to have to sleep with those same blankets that night.

She got ready, and we went downstairs for breakfast. We sat with some people from our group, but there was also a group from Germany on our table. We couldn't really talk with them because of the language barrier, but we exchanged pictures, and we still managed to have a good time.

We went to the training facility after breakfast. Mom and the other parents watched as we were introduced to our kung fu instructors. After we met everyone, we selected our weapons. There were swords, staffs, ball and chains, and fans. At the end of the trip we would know how to use all of them.

By the afternoon I was tired and sore. I'd suffered a few good whacks from the staff and from my sparring partner. We returned to the restaurant which had the sea turtle on the wall and served Peking duck. I only had a few bites though, because I couldn't stand looking at its head. Duck was the main dish, but there was also beef, chicken, tofu and veggies, and some stuff that I couldn't identify but ate anyway.

When we got back to the hotel, our room hadn't been cleaned. There was a note on the end table, but we couldn't read it, because it was in Chinese. I took it to the front desk to have it translated. I was so embarrassed when they told me what it said.

'We can't clean your room because it's too messy.'

If that wasn't bad enough, the lady thought *I* had wet the bed: 'If a child wets the bed, we need to be notified before you leave for the day so we can have clean sheets ready. Any further instances of bed wetting have to be called down to the front desk so we can take proper precautions.'

I couldn't believe they blamed me for the piss soaked sheets. That was my mom's fault, but because adults don't usually wet the bed, they blamed me. I told my mom what the note said and she started laughing.

'Oh, that's funny. They think you peed the bed. If they only knew.' she snorted.

'It's not funny. They started laughing when they came to that part. They think it was me when it was you. That's not fair,' I snapped. I was so angry.

Shaking her head, she said, 'These people will never see you again after this trip. It doesn't matter who they think peed the bed.'

I could feel the tears welling in my eyes.

'It matters to me,' I whimpered. I felt very sad all of a sudden.

We went swimming before bed. I wanted to soak in the hot tub, but the lifeguard wouldn't let me. Apparently kids under fifteen weren't allowed in.

When we went back to our hotel the room had been cleaned, but still I got hit in the face with the smell. The pong of the pee stung my eyes, making them water. We had only been there for a few days, but my mom's smell had already soaked the entire room. I quickly opened a window, trying to let in some fresh air. Nothing was going to help though, it had gone too far. It was weird seeing a clean room that smelled so bad.

• • •

Most of our time in China was spent training, but we also got to see some really cool places. We went to a jade factory where we saw workers hand carving figurines. I fell into a trance as I watched them cut so much detail into the stone, without a template. We also got to tour a silk factory and see the entire process, from the fat silk worms to the completed silk dresses.

The last place we toured was a fresh water pearl factory. When we first walked in, we each got to pick an oyster from a big tank in the middle of the floor. When we had all chosen one, we were taken to a large room with oyster shucking stations. We took a seat, and watched a video on how to extract the pearls. I had to ask for Mom's help with opening the oyster because I wasn't strong enough. When I opened it, there were so many pearls inside but I just felt sorry for them. They were like me, trapped inside a shell.

I was having so much fun hanging out with my friends, learning new techniques, and taking in the new culture, but every time we went back to the hotel I was thrown back into my problems at home. It was the worst feeling. Day by day, our once clean hotel room was morphing into our trash-filled house back home. Before we left for the day I would pick up any trash from the night before, quickly, while my mom was taking a shower. I stuffed her dirty clothes in a garbage bag and hid them in our empty suitcases. She seemed to wear enough clothes in one day for three people. We didn't get another note from management about the room being too messy. Mom peed the bed a few times during the trip, but it had always dried by the time we got back.

At the end of the week, eighty of us kids put on a performance to show off what moves we had learnt. I nervously huddled behind the curtain, waiting for the music to start playing. We were all lined up in rows, like race horses ready to run. The music started, and the curtain lifted. I was expecting to see everyone's parents, our instructors and a few others. I wasn't ready for hundreds of faces in the crowd watching. I was so nervous, I almost ran off the stage. But the kids around me starting the routine and I couldn't back down.

Even though there were hundreds of eyes watching, I still did a good job. I stayed in time with everyone else. I let out my shouts loud, and in time. Once I had got over the initial stage fright, I had a fun time.

We got back to the hotel after dinner and had a pool party. We kept getting in trouble because the pool's capacity was 100, but we had 120 people in our party. We didn't let that stop us from having fun though. We finally got chucked out of the pool area at 1 a.m. and split up into smaller groups, spending

a final night with each other before we parted
ways.

There must have been at least twenty of us in
one room. Everyone eventually crashed out, but
I couldn't fall asleep. I got up, cracked the window
open, and watched the world go by below me. I
didn't want to leave. Although Mom had turned
our hotel room into a stinking pigsty, I was still
having fun. I didn't want to go home. I knew what
was waiting for me when I got back – garbage,
mouldy laundry, dirty dishes and chores. Tears
started running down my cheeks. I didn't want to
wake anyone, but I couldn't hold back the sobs.
I buried my face into my arms to stifle the noise.

CHAPTER 10

'If you don't clean up the living room, I'll leave more fish livers in the bathtub,' Mom threatened. I was crying as I scurried into the living room, and started bagging up trash. I hated finding those gloopy red things where I washed. I hated it when Mom threatened me.

• • •

The alarm woke me from my dream. A dream about Mom's threats, from when I was little. I had hated finding those scary red blobs all over the house. I lay still for a moment, letting my heart slow from its frightened pounding.

I made my way to the bathroom. I turned on the shower to warm the water up, pulled down my pants and sat on the toilet. I shifted my weight, exposing the crotch of my panties. My heart dropped into my stomach. *Oh my God. That's what she was threatening me with all those years ago. I was* having my first period, my panties were soiled red, and in the gusset was a blood clot – a 'fish liver'.

I knew I was having a period because some of the girls in school had talked about it. Mom never bothered to explain stuff like that to me. I felt angry. I moved to the shower to let the hot water rush over me. *I can't believe she threatened me with fucking period blood*, I thought, punching the shower wall as hard as I could. The pain burned through my knuckles and the heat rose in my face. *Not only did she threaten me with her blood clots, but she left them for me to clean up*. I remembered finding fish livers on the couch, in the bathtub, on the floor.

After my shower I walked back to my room, but stopped in front of my mom's. I wanted her to know what was happening with me. Speaking loudly, so she would wake up, I said, 'Mom, I got my period today.'

She sounded like an elephant as she rolled over.

'Oh, kiddo. Thirteen years old and you're growing up. Do you need anything? There are pads under the sink,' she said, groggy from just waking up.

It was the first time I felt that I really hated my mom. I wanted to punch her in the face. *You're a disgusting, vile woman*. We had sanitary pads in the house, so why the hell didn't she use them? Why did she make me wipe up after her for all those years?

Not giving a shit what she said, I shrugged at her, grabbed a pad from under the sink, and went to my room to wait for the school bus to arrive. As I sat on my bed, I couldn't stop shuddering. Every time I closed my eyes, I could see the blobby fish livers in the bottom of the bath.

I saw the bus coming down the road. Grabbing my backpack, I flipped the lights off and raced downstairs. Just as I got outside, the bus had stopped at the end of the driveway. I ran over and hopped on, taking my usual seat. I was the third kid to be picked up, so I had nothing to do but think. Think about how my mom was a nasty, dirty woman. She ruined my trip to China by destroying my clean hotel room. She treated me like her slave, cleaning up her trash. But threatening me with her period blood. It was like the straw that broke the camel's back.

After school, I was tired so came straight home and did my chores and then my homework. I had some bad period cramps, so I lay down for a moment to ease the pain. When I woke up, it was pitch black outside. I checked my alarm clock – it was 3 a.m.! I rolled off the bed, still dressed in my school clothes. I peered in my mom's room – she was sleeping.

I clutched my painful stomach as I made my way towards the bathroom. Yuk, I stepped in something wet! I was so tired I kept going. I flipped on the light, sat down, and did my business.

Wiping the sleep from my eyes, I suddenly noticed there were a lot more puddles all over the floor. I cleaned myself up, and went to investigate where the puddles were coming from. There wasn't a leak in the ceiling, and the bathtub and the taps were turned off. I kicked the garbage with my bare feet, looking for an open bottle that might be leaking. I must have been too loud, because I could hear my mom stirring.

'Kiddo, it that you?' she asked, sleepily.

'Yeah. I thought you were going to wake me up when you got home. Now I'm not that tired,' I grumbled, still kicking garbage around.

My mom got up. Naked, as ever. I dodged to the side of the hallway so she could get past me on her way to the bathroom. As I watched her go by, I saw the existing puddles grow bigger, and new puddles forming. *Oh my God, I'm standing in a puddle of my mom's piss.* I jumped back in shock, falling over a pile of trash in the doorway.

'Whoa! Are you okay? What happened?' Mom yelled from the toilet.

I got up and angrily wiped my bare feet on a dirty shirt that was lying crumpled on the ground.

'I was just standing in a pool of your pee. Why the heck didn't you clean up after yourself?' I snapped. I couldn't hold back my anger anymore.

She burst out laughing.

'It's not a big deal. You don't usually wake up in the middle of the night and it usually evaporates before you get up,' she chuckled.

'Not a big deal. Not a big deal? You are so fat you can't even hold it in long enough to make it to the bathroom, and you think it's no big deal to just piss wherever you walk?' I screamed at her.

I'd had enough. I was reaching breaking point again. But Mom wasn't finished with me yet.

'*Don't* you use language like that, and don't even think about talking to me in that tone of voice again. Go to your room,' she yelled at me, while still on the toilet.

I stared disbelievingly at her through the open bathroom door. She looked pathetic, sitting there, naked, on the toilet. What was she going to do? Get up mid poop, and hit me in the face?

I took a deep breath. I jumped over the pools of piss and lay down on my bed, my face burning with anger.

I don't know how I managed to get back to sleep that night, but I woke up to my alarm a short while later. Before stepping into the hallway, I carefully looked for puddles of piss. There were a few, but I wasn't sure if they were new, or ones from earlier. I grabbed my shoes and slid them on, before going to the bathroom.

The next night, I woke up desperate to use the toilet, so I ran in my bare feet to the bathroom. As hard as I tried to avoid it, I still stepped on a shirt soaked with what I assumed to be pee. It was still warm, and squidgy between my toes. I dodged the other puddles and dived into the bathroom. On my way back to my bedroom I blindly made my way down the hallway, hoping to miss the landmines of pee. Relief – this time I was successful! I sat on the edge of my bed and wiped my feet off as best I could.

'I'm going to start wearing shoes to the bathroom all the time. This is fucking disgusting,' I muttered.

I felt like life had become about surviving rather than living. The first thing I did after school the next day was to make preparations for my night-time runs to the toilet. I dug a pair of flip-flops out from the sea of trash and placed them by my bedroom door. After that, I sat on the couch, and started homework. I didn't want to do my chores right away, so I decided I'd watch some TV and have a snack. I took three steps into the kitchen before the floor started to feel sticky. It was just like the back side of a Post-it note. Disgusted, I backed out of the kitchen. I wasn't sure if it was piss or some spilt drink, or rotting juices from old food. Truth be told, I didn't *want* to know what it was.

I grabbed the flip-flops I had just dug out, and wore them into the kitchen. With each step I could feel my flip-flops peeling off the ground. I grabbed some cinnamon Graham crackers to snack on and sat back down, taking my flip-flops off next to the couch. While munching on a cracker, I thought how I should wear shoes in the house all of the time. *Garbage won't stick to my feet, I won't step in piss and I don't have to worry what's caked on the kitchen carpet.*

When Mom got home she had some groceries she wanted help putting away. Instead of helping straight away, I looked for my flip-flops. I needed to protect my feet. Damn it, I had misplaced them! I was adamant I was not stepping foot into the kitchen without them though.

'I could really use your help,' Mom yelled from the kitchen, annoyed with me.

'I just have to find my flip-flops. I'm coming,'
I spluttered, as I found them in the nick of time,
under a pile of trash that had toppled over.

'Why do you need shoes to put groceries away?'
Mom asked, confused, as she rummaged through
the paper bags.

I was hesitant before answering her. If I said the
wrong thing, she would get mad.

'Um, well the floor is kind of sticky, and I didn't
like the feeling on my feet.' I mumbled.

Chuckling, she said, 'Oh get over it. It's not that
bad. I walk barefoot in here all the time.'

I didn't reply. Instead I quietly put the groceries
away, noticing that the floor was at its stickiest in
front of the fridge and the oven.

I grabbed the bag of food Mom had got for me
from work and went through to the living room.
Mom had already stripped off and was sitting naked
on the couch. Her work clothes were in a heap, just
in front of her, her takeaway container on her knee.
Looking at her, I couldn't believe how she managed
to hold down a good job in a kitchen. That they
allowed her near food. Yet here we were, about to
tuck into her hospital lasagne, chips and corn.

• • •

At school the next day, a friend we sometimes ate lunch with handed out invitations to her thirteenth birthday party sleepover.

'These are basically for show for your parents. My mom and dad are going to get us some booze and the boys don't actually have to leave. My parents will cover for everyone so don't worry. Let me know tomorrow if you guys can come because it's this weekend. Oh, and they'll bring everyone home,' Misty explained to everyone at the table.

Everyone was excited, except for Nancy and me. On our walk home after school, we talked about the party.

'Well, I know I'm not going to be able to spend the night, my curfew is midnight on Saturdays. I'll just have to leave a bit earlier,' Nancy said, kicking a rock across our path.

'My mom will probably let me spend the night if her parents are going to cover for us like that. I'm just nervous because I've never drank, except for the little bit my mom and grandma let me sip from their drinks,' I said, nervously.

We stopped by Nancy's house, and I helped her with her chores. I didn't mind because it meant we could hang out longer, instead of me waiting for her to get them done. And her chores were things like wiping down the surfaces and putting away the dishes – which were very different to the sort of chores I had to do. It was a nice feeling to see something clean at the end of all that hard work. In our house, no matter how much you cleaned, it was still dirty.

At the hospital, I showed my mom the party invite. I couldn't tell if she was in a nice or nasty mood.

'Can I go this weekend? They'll bring me home. And you can call them to confirm everything,' I said, pointing to their phone number. I braced myself for the bad news.

'I'll call them after work, but I don't see why not,' she said, pinning the invitation on her notice board.

'Awesome, thanks Mom.' I couldn't believe she had said yes. It helped me forget all the bad stuff that had happened that week.

• • •

I couldn't wait for Misty's birthday party. On Saturday, it was the only thing I could talk about. We picked Nancy up at 4.30 p.m. and headed over to Misty's house. When we got there, her parents greeted us at the door with party hats. Mom came inside to meet Misty's parents, just to make sure everything was okay. Nancy and I headed downstairs where the party was taking place.

After a few minutes, Mom shouted down the stairs, 'Bye Britney, see you tomorrow.'

'Bye mom,' I replied, embarrassed to have my mom fussing over me.

After about thirty minutes everyone had arrived. We hung out like we normally would – watching anime, reading manga and listening to music. Pizza finally arrived, and everyone scoffed them down. It doesn't take long for ten kids to finish off a stack of pizza. At 10 p.m., Misty's parents called everyone to come upstairs. They handed out mixed drinks and beer, while Misty opened her presents. She got a whole bunch of new mangas, a scarf and matching hat, and a couple of DVDs.

'Britney, I have to be home in a little bit, and I can't be drunk. But I also don't want to be made fun of for not drinking,' Nancy whispered in my ear.

'You're not going to be made fun of for not drinking, you know that,' I whispered back.

'Well, Troy was making fun of me for it earlier,' she said, sadly.

'If that's the case, then take a drink, and sit on it for a while. Make it seem like you're drinking a lot even though it's not that much,' I handed her a beer.

She popped the top and took a sip. She shook her head in disgust, and spluttered.

'I don't have to worry about getting drunk. This shit's nasty,' she said laughing.

I kept drinking, while Nancy sipped on her beer. At 11.30 p.m. she gave me a hug, and left for home. Everyone kept knocking the drinks back as we watched more anime. At two or three in the morning, Misty's older brother Cam came home. He was just a few years older than us, and all of the girls instantly had a crush on him.

He headed downstairs to where we were and grabbed two beers. He chugged the first one. The second beer he sipped on for a while. After their parents went to bed, Jason, her other brother, pulled a bag of green stuff out of his pocket.

'Anyone wanna smoke weed?' He asked, breaking it up on a DVD case.

Troy, Alana and Misty were all onboard. A couple of the other kids and I were hesitant, however. He sat there breaking up the weed until it was very fine, almost powdery. He then pulled out a little orange pack of papers. He took a sheet, put what looked to be too much weed on it, and rolled it into a joint. He lit it, puffed on it a few times, then handed it to Troy.

Troy, Misty and Alana each took a few hits off the joint. As they were hitting it, Misty's brother started rolling another joint. Alana held out the joint to me. I looked at Amy, a girl who was hesitant about smoking too, and shrugged. I took the joint and hit it.

I could feel the smoke fill my lungs. My chest was on fire. I coughed – I couldn't stand it any longer. Even though there was no smoke in my lungs anymore, they still burned. I couldn't stop coughing, my eyes were watering – I couldn't catch my breath. Amy didn't hit the joint, she just passed it.

By the time I got my breath back, the second joint was passed around to me. This time I took a smaller hit, inhaling cautiously. It still burnt my lungs, but it wasn't as bad. I stood up to pass the joint on to the next person. Whoa, I was really light-headed. The room started to spin, I felt high.

I lay back down, enjoying the feeling. I wasn't drunk because I didn't like how the alcohol had made me feel. I had stopped drinking a few hours before. But the feeling of being high was amazing. It was like nothing I'd ever experienced. Someone hit me on the shoulder, and dangled the joint in front of my face again. I opened my mouth, and whoever passed the joint, put it in my mouth. I filled up with smoke and grunted, letting whoever it was know I was done with it. They took the joint, and I sunk back.

I let the smoke take over my body. I held my breath wanting to keep this moment forever. The next thing I remember was waking up to the sun pouring in the windows. I looked around and everyone was passed out all over the place. Troy and Alana were sleeping next to each other in the corner.

I went to the bathroom, and when I got back, everyone was starting to wake up. Jason was already breaking up more weed. Instead of putting it in papers, this time he pulled out a vase looking thing. It had a little stem, which he put some weed into. Jason put his mouth on the top opening, lit the stem of weed so it was on fire and inhaled. He took a deep breath and slumped into the chair.

'Wanna hit this shit?' he coughed.

'Yeah, how do I do it?' I asked, sitting down next to him.

'Just inhale up here; light this, and when the bong is charged with smoke, pull the stem out and inhale. If it's your first time hitting a bong though, it might be killer on your lungs.'

I hit the bong like he showed me, pulled the stem out and took a deep breath. I started coughing instantly. It was like the smoke was a hundred times more concentrated than the joint smoke. I started gagging because I couldn't breathe. Jason patted me on my back, trying to help me. I finally caught my breath, but my head was swimming. The high was more intense. All of my problems seemed to vanish. I felt like I was light as a feather, floating up through the clouds to a place where I didn't have to fight so hard to survive.

Misty's parents shouted downstairs that they would be giving everyone a lift in an hour and that we should get ready to go. I didn't have anything to pack up so a bunch of us sat in a circle hitting the bong and smoking joints, rolled by Jason. It seemed like only a few minutes passed before we had to leave. I was super giggly walking to the car.

When we got to my house, I stumbled out of the car, still high. Before I unlocked the door, I took a deep breath, trying to regain my composure. *I can't let Mom know.* I opened the door and yelled, 'Hey Mom. I'm home.'

I staggered up the stairs but missed the first step a couple of times. I started giggling uncontrollably. My mom opened the upstairs door.

'What is going on? Why are you so happy?' she shouted down.

I almost said 'Because I'm high', but I stopped myself.

'I'm just happy from staying up all night,' I laughed.

I walked upstairs and sat on the couch. Looking at the trash didn't seem so bad now that I was high. Yes, it sucked that it was crazy messy, but I wasn't in a state of mind to care. I stuck my hand in my pocket, and fingered the bud of weed Jason had given me. *I'll smoke it after school on Monday. Mom won't be home, and I don't have to give a fuck about this house anymore.*

CHAPTER 11

It was a day when I went straight home from school, and I was still picking up trash when I heard the door downstairs open.

'Hey Mom. How was work?' I went down to greet her.

'Terrible. Now move,' she snarled, as she stomped past, like an elephant.

I dodged to the side, and started explaining what chores I had finished. I was really proud of myself because I had done more than she had asked, and I had also completed my homework. She cut me off mid-sentence.

'You know what? I don't care. These are things you're supposed to do,' she spat.

I felt crushed because I was proud of what I had accomplished.

'Okay, well why was work that bad? What happened that made it so terrible?' I tried to make things better. I followed her into the kitchen with my flip-flops on.

She swung around to face me.

'Stop talking to me. Okay?' she said in a pissed off tone.

Confused, I took a step back.

'But why? What did I do?' I quivered.

Mom shook her head and massaged her temples.

'I don't know. But I just want to fight with you. That's what mothers and daughters do.'

What? Why does Mom want to hurt me? I was angry and upset, I couldn't understand her reasoning.

'That's stupid. I haven't done anything to make you mad, so you have no right to be mad at me,' I said.

Pointing her chubby finger in my face she said, 'Don't you fucking tell me. Now go to your room.'

I ran to my room and dived onto my bed. *God, I wish I had a door to slam*, I thought to myself. After I cooled off a bit, I started crying. *Why does she want to fight with me? That's bullshit*, I thought, stifling my cries into my pillow.

I was so distraught, I started running over the past couple of months in my head, looking for some sort of explanation. *What have I done to make Mom want to fight with me?* I had been doing all of the chores she'd asked of me, and I'd been doing okay in my classes in school. I had mostly As and only a few Bs. Some days I would hate my mom with such a vengeance I could punch a wall. But then I would feel guilty for having these feelings. More than anything though, I just wanted her to love me and be proud of me. That's why I tried so hard to do the things she asked of me.

I decided that she would like me more if I worked harder in school and if I did even more chores. I thought up a system that would make me be a better daughter.

Every day over the next month was dedicated to pleasing my mom. I stopped hanging out with Nancy after school, and instead went straight home. Tennis season had come to a close, and kung fu was only one night a week.

First thing I did after stepping through the door was put a load of laundry on. I then called Mom. As I talked with her I would start picking up a bag of trash. By the time a couple of bags were full, it would be time to get another wash on. After that, I'd start my homework – which I'd already begun on the bus ride home. The whole while I'd listen intently to the washer, waiting for it to stop. When the second load was done, I'd stop studying and start a third load. I'd pick up more garbage until I ran out of trash bags. I heaved the full trash bags down the stairs onto the porch, where they would fester until my mom was ready to take them over to my aunt's or my grandma's house. I now knew we did this because Mom was cheap – she didn't want to pay for her own trash collection, so she used her family to help us out. I never heard Grandma say anything about it, but I can't imagine she was happy with Mom always freeloading from her.

I tried so hard, but nothing seemed to please my mom anymore. Her 'nice days' were few and far between. I was doing way more chores than she had asked, but Mom was still always angry with me. The nastier she was with me, the more I tried to make her love me. I was trapped in some vicious circle.

After a month, Mom increased my chore load again.

'If you can do all of this, you most definitely can do more,' she said.

I tried explaining that I'd done as much as I could, but she wouldn't listen. She walked in one day, saw that there was a load of laundry still going, and asked, 'So how much laundry have you done?'

I let her know that it was the fourth load. Her blankets had to be washed every day and they didn't all fit in one load. Mom didn't care. She lost it.

'I can't believe you've only done four loads. We have a hell of a lot more laundry than that!' she yelled.

I desperately tried to explain that I'd timed the washer, and four loads was all I could do from the time I got home from school to the time she arrived home from work. My pleas fell on deaf ears. She screamed at me, saying it wasn't good enough. She said I wasn't 'doing good' with my chores anymore. She banned me from hanging out with Nancy. My escape from home, my best friend, was taken away from me. I would only be able to see Nancy during lunch now because we didn't have any classes together.

Yet the more Mom hurt me, the more I wanted to please her. I stopped my half hour study time so I could do more chores. After a few weeks, my grades started slipping. Not only was I getting in trouble for not doing a good enough job with my chores, but now Mom was shouting at me for my bad grades. I got my first C on a test, and she grounded me for a month and banned me from watching TV. She uninstalled the satellite television and would leave the remote in a certain position, and on a certain channel, so she'd know if I had watched TV or not. I got caught the first day and had an extra week added to my grounding. I was so burnt out from studying and cleaning, I was losing the will to live.

• • •

Nancy tried to cheer me up one lunch time, but it was no good.

'Hey, my birthday party is next weekend. I'll see you there,' she beamed.

'Um, I don't know if I'll be able to make it. My mom's been a bitch lately,' I said, pushing the food around on my tray.

'You know she'll let you come. It's me after all,' she said, giving me a side hug.

Leaning in to her hug, I said, 'I hope so.'

When Mom got home from work, I was hesitant about asking her if I could go to Nancy's birthday party. It didn't seem to matter what I said, she was always mad at me. During a commercial break on TV, I got her a can of her favourite soda to sweeten her up.

'Nancy is having her birthday party next weekend. Can I go?' I asked, handing it to her.

She cracked the seal on the can, and took a big slurp. 'Well, how did you do on your science test? And did you do all of your chores?'

My heart started pounding. I was nervous that she could hear it. Looking at the floor, I said, 'I got a B on my science test. And I got most of my chores done, but I also had homework and—'

'And that means you didn't get an A, and you didn't finish your chores. If you keep this shit up you're not going,' she snapped, her gaze never leaving the TV.

Getting up, I whispered, 'Okay. I'll do better.'

As I was walking away, she snarled, almost under her breath, 'You better.'

Downstairs, I changed the load of laundry. The dryer was still going so I had to take the wet stuff from the washer and hang it out across anything I could rest it on, in the basement. We didn't have any clothes horses. *I've got five loads washed before Mom gets home, but she still doesn't understand that that's the best I can do. I can't do any more, I can't cope.*

The next day at school, I broke the news to Nancy that I probably couldn't come.

'That's stupid. Doesn't she realise that you got the third best grade in the class on that test? It was a hard one,' she huffed.

My head was now buried in my folded arms. In a muffled voice, I said, 'She doesn't understand. I'm not doing as well as her when she was my age.'

I could hear Nancy rummaging through her backpack. 'Well, I have something that will cheer you up,' she said, setting down something heavy on the dinner table. Everyone at the table gasped in unison, and Alana let out a loud squeal.

I lifted my head just enough to see what was on the table. There were chocolate, strawberry and vanilla Pocky boxes. I quickly reached out, grabbing the vanilla one. As I was tearing open the box, Nancy said, 'My dad brought these back for me from his trip to Chicago. I couldn't believe he found these. Usually you have to go to a Japanese grocery store just to find the chocolate ones, and yet he got the others too.'

Pocky boxes and foil wrappers littered our table, as everyone munched on the candy-dipped crackers. I laid one of each in front of me, wanting to savour the moment. Pocky is so hard to find, especially the flavoured ones. I picked up the pink one, examining the long thin cracker dipped in strawberry chocolate. I took a bite and let it melt in my mouth. I was surprised – it didn't taste like artificial strawberry, but real fruit.

I finished the strawberry stick and started to eat the vanilla one. Nancy tapped my arm and slid a CD out of her hoodie pocket.

'I made this for you last night. It's got twenty-three songs on it, ranging from J-pop to rock, to rap, to even a country song,' she said, with a big smile on her face.

She took so much time making it for me. She designed a cover using pictures of the two of us from over the past year, and she even had a song list on the back. As I was slipping it into my bag, Nancy said, 'You have to open it.'

I gave her a confused look, and popped open the CD case. On the CD was a picture someone took of Nancy and me, hugging each other on a bench, taken from behind us. The top edge had the words 'Best Friends' written in fancy bubble letters.

I gave her a big hug and couldn't stop thanking her. I felt so bad that I'd never given her anything that meaningful. She loved the jade bracelet that I'd brought her back from China, but I hadn't put as much thought into it as this. And it was *her* birthday that was coming up!

'What prompted this?' I asked, still looking the CD over.

'Well, your mom is being a bitch and not letting you hang out with me. I miss you, so I did this to pass the time,' she said, picking up the Pocky trash.

I'd never had a real friend before. I could feel my eyes welling up with tears of happiness.

• • •

After school, Nancy tracked me down before I got on the bus.

'Hey, I had an idea. What if you told your mom you missed the bus? Then we could hang out,' she said, being really bubbly.

Scratching the back of my head, and looking ahead at my bus, I said, 'I don't know. She might get really mad. I get in a lot of trouble if I miss the bus in the morning, I think she'll be mad if I miss it after school.'

Nancy mulled it over for a second.

'She's only mad because she has to go out of the way to bring you to school in the morning. After school you're waiting on her. She shouldn't be mad. Come on Britney, it's video game night at the library,' Nancy pushed.

'Okay, okay. But I need to call her in a little bit to let her know I missed the bus,' I said, walking away from my ride home.

'Just call from my house. Let's go,' she urged, heading towards our normal route through the woods.

We got to Nancy's house and made sure her parents weren't home. We went inside, and I called my mom.

'Um, hey Mom,' I said nervously.

'Wow, you're calling really early. Was there no traffic?' she asked.

'Um, well, no. I asked my teacher for help after school and I ended up missing the bus,' I lied.

After a long pause, my mom shouted: 'Are you fucking serious? There's shit at home that needs to be done. It's trash night, we need to make sure to run that shit over to your grandparents' house.'

'I, I'm sorry. I needed help with math after school. I didn't—'

She cut me off mid-sentence. 'There's always lunch. There's no reason for you to miss the fucking bus. You know what? Just get over to the hospital as quick as possible so I can run you home,' she said, then she hung up.

I put the phone back on its base, and slumped down into the kitchen chair. Nancy was doing chores, and noticed my desolate face.

'Uh oh. How did that call go?' she asked, sitting down across from me.

Not looking her in the eyes, I said. 'She's crazy mad. I've got to get going.'

I grabbed my backpack and reluctantly headed for the door.

'Well, wait for me to get my chores done and I'll come with,' she said, grabbing the broom and sweeping.

'No, you won't want to be there. She's pissed; she won't let me go with you.'

Nancy ran to the door as I was stepping out.

'Britney, I'm so sorry. If I knew your mom was going to get that mad I wouldn't have pressured you,' she said, giving me a hug.

'Don't worry,' I said, squeezing her back. I closed my eyes for a moment, then pulled away. I grimaced. 'Time to face the music.'

• • •

When I got to the hospital I hung outside the kitchen door for a while, nervous about facing my mom. I took a deep breath, and opened the door. She was at her station with a large knife, cutting green peppers. I knew she would never use it on me, but it made me uneasy nonetheless.

'Hi Mom,' I said, cautiously.

Not looking up from what she was doing she said, 'I can't believe you missed the bus. I work my ass off for us and you can't even do something simple like your chores.'

She started chopping the green peppers more feverishly. I didn't say anything because I didn't know what to say, and I'd learnt it was better to just keep quiet. Suddenly she stopped.

'Well?' she said, tossing the knife onto the counter.

'Um, I needed help with algebra. You know I jumped a math class. I'm a year ahead of my peers and it gets hard sometimes,' I said, fiddling with the zipper on my hoodie.

Mocking me she mimicked, '"I'm a year ahead of my peers, it gets hard sometimes."' She shook her head, picked up the knife, and resumed chopping. 'If it's that hard, maybe I should take you out of that class.'

'No,' I said, panicking. I'd worked so hard to get in that class. I was really proud that I applied myself, and I managed to keep an A average. I even did my summer homework, which nobody likes to do.

'I can't even talk with you anymore. Go do your homework and don't bother me until it's time to go,' she hissed.

I grabbed a drink and started my homework. When I was done, I began studying for my history and math tests, which were coming up. It felt good to study and not be cooped up in that awful house. I felt like I was doing something productive instead of drowning in trash.

• • •

When we got home, Mom made me start a load of laundry, and pick up as many bags of garbage as possible. She, on the other hand, sat on her ass at the computer, browsing the internet. As I was picking her trash up, she kept stopping me from throwing things away, reasoning that it still had value or we could use it later. There was no pattern to what she wanted to keep and throw away. Mouldy takeaway dishes could go, but shoes with holes in them could stay. Mom had brought home a bag full of second-hand clothes that were not even in her size – they had to stay. Of course the newspapers had to stay – that was a given. I threw a soggy book on a pile of moth-eaten clothes, newspapers and single shoes.

After what seemed like forever, Mom decided that I had picked up enough trash to haul to my grandparents' house and told me to take the bags downstairs. The ones from the kitchen were leaking a foul smelling liquid.

'Mom, what should I do with these? They're leaking,' I asked, holding the bag as far away as my arm could reach.

Not looking up from the computer she said, 'Well, they sure as hell aren't staying in the house.'

I picked up another bag, carried them downstairs, and loaded them into the car. On trash nights we couldn't fit much into the car, because there was so much crap already stuffed in it.

Before I put the leaking bags in the car, I made sure none of my stuff was underneath it. I even went as far as to put some of my mom's clothes under the leak. It didn't matter, because I was the one to wash the clothes anyway.

Out of breath, I said, 'Okay, we can go.'

The car was so full you couldn't see out of the back window, and I had a bag of trash at my feet and on my lap. I felt so disgusting, sitting in a heap of garbage, but I didn't have a choice. Pulling out of the driveway, I shifted my weight because I was uncomfortable.

'Don't let the bags rustle like that. I hate that noise, especially while driving,' Mom snapped.

I didn't answer. I just rolled my eyes and thought, *Try being the one to sit in this shit.*

After twenty minutes we were finally at my grandparents'. We parked outside where the rubbish bin was. It was already half full, so we were going to have to leave bags around the bin. I opened the door, and tossed the bag on my lap onto the ground. A glass jar inside shattered, breaking the silence of the night.

My mom hushed at me.

'Be careful, anything that gets out of the bag you'll have to pick up,' she threatened.

'I know,' I said, stretching my legs.

We filled the rubbish bin and had several bags in a neat pile next to it, but we still had a few more bags in the car. My mom went down the road and found a neighbour's bin half full.

'Hop in. We're going to put the rest of this in a bin down the road,' she said, pulling over, right next to the bin.

I looked at her as if she was crazy. I knew this was wrong. One thing was to freeload from our family, but not from a poor neighbour.

'Hurry up,' Mom revved the car.

I didn't want to be caught, so I ran with bags in both hands. My heart was galloping as I slung them into the neighbour's bin. I sprinted back to the car and shouted, 'Go!'

She sped off and I shrunk into my seat with embarrassment.

• • •

The torture continued. I was grounded for missing the bus after school – and my mom didn't let me go to Nancy's birthday party. I was really upset because I had made us matching friendship bracelets in our favourite colours. Hers was red and black, and mine was blue and black. I also got her a new pair of headphones.

The next day Mom went to the store to grab some soda. As soon as the car left the driveway, I quickly rang Nancy.

'Hey, how was your party?' I whispered.

'It was okay. I wish you could have been there. Why are you whispering?' she asked, confused.

Talking normally again, I said, 'Because I'm grounded and not allowed to use the phone. She's at the store right now, but I guess I was nervous.'

'You're silly. Well I have to go, I still have guests,' she groaned.

'Okay, happy birthday. Bye,' I said. I felt very sad.

• • •

On Monday I was excited to get back to school. I wanted to give Nancy her presents, and I couldn't wait to hang out with her at lunch. I sat at the table talking with everyone else, only half paying attention to what they had to say as I waited for her to arrive. The bell rang, but Nancy never showed up. I called her after school and discovered her grandparents were in town so she'd been pulled out of school. I missed my friend.

I felt uneasy when I got home that night. I called Mom to let her know I was back, and asked for my chore list. Instead, she started yelling at me about my grades.

'I checked online and it says you have a zero on a lot of your assignments in several classes. What the fuck is that about? Why aren't you doing homework?' she snapped.

'Online grades are a new thing,' I tried to explain. 'My teachers have put zeroes in the boxes to let themselves know what they still need to input. I really have As in those classes, but it looks like a D, because of the zeroes,' I said, almost pleading with her.

Snorting, she said, 'That's bullshit. Because you're not responsible enough I'm going to go through all of your homework at the end of the night.'

'That's fine, because I do my homework. It's just not in the online system yet. It'll get updated in a few days,' I said, hurt at what she just said.

'You don't need to lie. You just need to start doing your fucking homework,' she shouted.

I gave up.

'You can start looking at my homework. It'll be done,' I mumbled, defeated.

Taking a breath of disbelief, she said, 'I can start looking at your homework? So now I need your permission? I'm the fucking parent, you're the child. Learn your place.'

Struggling for words, I spluttered, 'That's not what I meant. It was more like "feel free to look". I don't have an attitude or anything. I'm just letting you know I actually do my homework.'

'You know what? I'm done, we'll pick this up when I get home. Now I need you to wash my blankets. They're soaked and I don't want to sleep on them wet again. Also, you need to pick up the trash in the kitchen. There is a whole bunch of food rubbish in the sink. Now repeat what you have to do,' she ordered.

'Uh, um. I have to wash your blankets and pick up garbage in the kitchen,' I said quietly.

'And the food garbage in the sink,' she said in an annoyed tone.

I could hear someone calling my mom's name in the background.

'I've got to go. Chores and homework must be done. If you have any downtime you can pick up more shit,' and she hung up.

I started a load of laundry, trying my best not to touch the parts she had pissed on. When I got upstairs I immediately started emptying the kitchen sink. It was disgusting. There were avocado peels and pits, egg shells, mouldy bowls and a whole bunch of unidentifiable stuff festering in there.

I held my breath, and put a grocery bag over my hand so I didn't have to touch anything nasty.

I picked up a bowl, half full of mould. When I poured it into the trash bag it was thick and took some time sliding out the side. I shook it a few times to try and loosen the sludge. The mould on top split open and revealed hundreds of maggots squirming around. Startled, I dropped the bowl in the trash bag.

That's when I started crying. My knees buckled and I stumbled to the living room, to sit down. *No matter what I do, it isn't good enough. I'm worthless. Mom thinks I'm lying all the time, but I'm not. It's not my fault the teachers aren't familiar with the new online grading system, and it's not my fault she gives me more chores than I can do.*

Breathing started getting harder. I leaned forwards, putting my head between my knees, focusing on my breath. When I opened my eyes all I saw was the garbage at my feet. Chocolate bar wrappers, dirty silverware, dirty clothes, dirt, bugs. This was my life – living in filth.

I can't do this anymore, I thought, getting up and heading for the bathroom. I started rifling through the medicine cabinet for any pills I could find.

I'm not going to be dumb and try to suffocate myself. This time I'm doing it right.

I felt calm. In fact, I was happy. I wasn't going to have to deal with the house or my mom anymore. I was almost excited. *Who knows? The afterlife could be super fun.* I was happy I wouldn't have to feel worthless anymore. The prospect of not feeling anything ever again enticed me a lot.

I took seven pills from each bottle, and shoved them in my pocket. We only had a few prescriptions in our medicine cabinet, but I figured that the amount of pills, and the combination of pills, would do the trick. I went to the kitchen, and grabbed the bottle of raspberry vodka that was wedged between the fridge and the counter.

I'd found the bottle a while ago under some garbage. I had hidden it so I could take a sip every once in a while when things got too bad. I rinsed off a Styrofoam cup I had found on the floor, and filled it halfway with the vodka. I put the bottle back, because for some reason I didn't want my mom finding me surrounded by drug packets and a bottle of vodka.

I sat on the couch and tried taking a small handful of tablets all at the same time. I took a swig of vodka, and almost choked on the amount of pills combined with the burning of the vodka. I spat everything out into my hands, and decided it would be best to take the pills one at a time. One by one, I put a tablet in my mouth, took a mouthful of vodka and swallowed. My throat burned each time.

I had a few pills left when I started to feel dizzy. I quickly finished the last of them off, and then finished the last bit of vodka. Before I got too messed up, I got up, and rinsed out the cup so it didn't smell like alcohol.

On my way back to the couch, the room started spinning. I was ready for the peace to wash over me, I just needed to sit down. I was almost at the couch when I tripped over my backpack. My presents for Nancy fell out of the front pocket. I scrambled to my feet, grabbing the bracelets and the headphones, before sitting down.

I couldn't see anymore, the colours of our bracelets had melted together. I started crying. I was going to miss Nancy and wished I'd had a chance to say goodbye.

• • •

The next thing I knew, my mom was shaking me and slapping my face.

'Britney! Britney! What's going on? Are you okay?' she said in a panicked tone.

I opened my droopy eyes and saw I was lying in a pool of vomit.

'Oh thank God. Let's sit you up.' She grabbed my shoulders and pulled me up, propping me against the corner of the couch.

'What did you eat at school? You've got food poisoning,' she asked, feeling my forehead.

Before I could answer I threw up again all over the floor. Odd as it may sound, I suddenly became aware that I hadn't died. I scanned the piles of vomit looking for half-digested pills. *I'll just grab them before she notices.*

Mom tried to get me to stand, but I couldn't even sit up. She grabbed a towel and laid it over the puke puddle on the couch. She coaxed me to lie down.

'Not on your back. If you pass out again you could drown,' she said, propping a pillow behind me.

Perfect. I thought, trying to fight her off. I was so weak, though, that she easily won.

She grabbed Nancy's presents out of my hand.

'We don't want those to get messy now. You worked so hard on them.'

She took a blanket and tucked me in, pulling my shoes and socks off. Weakly, I asked, 'So you're not mad at me?'

She sat on the edge of the couch, and gently stroked my cheek.

'Of course not. You've got food poisoning and are obviously dehydrated. I'm going to keep an eye on you, but you should be fine,' she said, kindly.

I don't think she had a clue what I had just done. She was so wrapped up in herself.

● ● ●

I woke up the next day when it was light outside. I had a headache from hell, and my body was sore all over. I started panicking, *Oh my God. I missed the bus. I'm in such deep shit.* I got up, and stepped in the pile of puke next to the couch.

'Eww,' I said, loudly.

I jumped when Mom yelled from the other side of the house. 'Kiddo, is that you?'

'Yeah. I'm so sorry I missed the bus. I just—'

Stopping me mid-sentence, she said, 'Don't worry about it. You're staying home today and tomorrow. You had a gnarly case of food poisoning. You need to drink lots of water today while I'm at work. And eat if you can.'

But I don't want to fucking be here. That's why I tried killing myself, I thought, almost breaking down in tears.

'You need to relax and focus on getting better. You'll go back to school on Friday if you're feeling up to it. I've already called the school.'

I nodded my head and traipsed back to my room. I waited for Mom to turn the shower on before I screamed into my pillow, 'Stupid, stupid, stupid! You're a failure at life *and* at death!'

PART 3

CHAPTER 12

Nancy and I went to freshman orientation together, so we could get a feel for our new school. I couldn't believe I was about to start high school. It was huge, all of the middle school students in the district transferred here. We were given lockers, and I put my books, backpack and gym clothes in mine, so they'd be clean and organised for my first day.

Nancy and I celebrated my fourteenth birthday before school started. A carnival was in town, so I searched the rubbish in Mom's car for loose change so we could play some of the games and get some food. I got enough money to keep us entertained for a few hours. Even though it was still summer break, it was rare that I was allowed hang out with Nancy. Only on special occasions or a on few scattered days when my mom was in a good mood.

• • •

School was starting the next day. Mom offered to give me and Nancy a ride, and before I thought about it I said yes and gave Nancy a call. It was only when I hung up that I realised that the car needed to be cleaned, badly. I'd been trying to keep the legroom in the front seat somewhat clear, not letting bottles overrun, but the back seat was horrendous. There were old takeaway boxes, crumpled fast food bags, half full bottles of soda, garage sale hauls that had yet to be brought inside, and even more junk.

I easily filled two bags of trash from the back seat, and tossed them in the garage to wait for the next trash run to Grandma's. I dumped the stuff from the garage sales in the laundry room. It took up a good bit of space in the car, but only added a few inches to one pile of many in the laundry room. I stopped emptying out the car when I had just enough leg space.

The next morning, I quickly hopped out of the front passenger seat so Nancy didn't have to sit in the back with the garbage. By now she was used to how the car smelled and looked. I'd still never let her near the house.

'I'm so glad we finally have classes together,' she said, looking over at me.

Smiling, I said, 'I know! I can't believe our schedules lined up so perfectly.'

When we got to the high school, I went to my locker to grab my backpack and drop off all of the things Mom had made me take along. She had sent me to school with several water bottles, a change of clothes, extra pads and tampons, and a bunch of granola bars. I didn't want to take the time organizing everything, so I just dumped it all in the bottom of my locker, filling it up halfway.

Nancy and I made our way to the cafeteria, where her older brother and sister liked to hang out with their friends. I felt cool because we were sitting with seniors and nobody made fun of us. I felt so mature being able to hold a conversation with them.

The bell rang, and Nancy and I parted ways – we didn't have a class together until second period. Looking at my schedule, I realised I had left my textbook in my locker and I would need it for class. I rushed back, and when I opened up the locker, some of the stuff I had jammed in the bottom fell out. A teacher, walking by, spoke in a stern voice, 'That's a bad habit to get into. Especially at the beginning of the year.'

'Excuse me?' I asked, picking the stuff up off the floor.

'You're hoarding rubbish in your locker. You don't usually see that until winter rolls around,' she said, crossing her arms.

Shoving the stuff back into my locker, I explained, 'Oh no. I just didn't have time to organize it. I'll do it tomorrow before school.'

I grabbed my book, shut my locker and started heading to class. As I was weaving between the desks, the realisation suddenly hit me, *Oh my God. Mom is a 'hoarder'.*

I knew there were hoarders in the world, but I'd always just thought my mom was very lazy. I sat still as a statue as my new knowledge settled. I didn't pay attention to anything that was being said around me. Classmates were being introduced, desks were being organised, but I was too busy trying to rack my brain for any information I had about hoarders. All I knew was that they wouldn't throw things away and their houses were piled high with trash. Nancy and I got seats next to each other in our second class. Before it started, I leaned over and whispered, 'Hey. I think my mom's a hoarder.'

'Duh. Have you seen her car?' she laughed.

'Yeah, I just never thought about it,' I said, pretending to laugh it off.

God, if only Nancy knew what our house looked

like. We had been best friends for three years and I had never let her set foot inside my house.

The rest of the day went by in a blur. I couldn't wait to get the bus home and look up the definition of a hoarder. Maybe there was help out there for Mom. I skipped my chores, and raced over to the computer to look it up on the internet.

I typed 'hoarder definition' into the search bar. I sat back, and took a deep breath, as I read it out loud:

Hoarding is the excessive collection of items, along with the inability to discard them. Hoarding often creates such cramped living conditions that homes may be filled to capacity, with only narrow pathways winding through stacks of clutter.

I looked around me to examine the evidence. To the left of me was a pile of newspapers as high as my waist. To the right of me were piles of old clothes that were riddled with holes and mould clusters. Between the newspapers and the clothes were dozens of food and takeaway wrappings. Our house matched the description in the dictionary – perfectly.

I took a big gulp of air – I hadn't realised I'd been holding my breath the whole time out of shock.

I shook my head with despair. I almost wished I hadn't made my discovery, because I didn't know what to do with it. That familiar feeling of blaming myself for not trying hard enough returned.

What do I do now? If I try to get help, they will blame me. They will say I'm fourteen, and old enough to clean the house. They wouldn't understand. It's not just about throwing things away; it's about fighting with my mom over what is trash and what is for keeping.

There was a column suggesting some local support groups, but I knew I could never get Mom to attend those. And I was scared about what would happen to me. I knew about the care system and how kids can be taken away from their parents. I didn't want that to be me. I hated Mom for making me live like an animal, but she was my mom at the end of the day. I loved her.

So I brushed my discovery under the carpet, just like all the rest of the trash in our house.

• • •

I tried to forget about my problems by making myself look good for my second day at school. In my bedroom mirror, I fixed my hair so it looked good down and put on some make-up. I drew on black eyeliner and painted my lips bright red. My eyebrows were hidden by my new black, thick-rimmed glasses. I had had another recent revelation – I'd decided in middle school that there was no way I was ever going to school again with holes and stains in my clothes. Now, from my new dressing table, I reached for my neatly folded black band T-shirt and cut-off denim shorts, and put them on over colourful leggings. I topped it off with my black sneakers.

I was slouched in my usual seat on the bus, picked up kids for all the schools in the area, listening to my MP3 player, when we stopped at a new house. A younger girl bounced up the stairs. She had blonde hair but her fringe was dyed pink.

A few seconds later, a guy bounded up the stairs after her. He was very tall, at least six foot. He was wearing a black leather jacket over a map of Illinois T-shirt. His trousers were black, and rolled up to mid-calf. He had a red bandana tied around his left thigh. To top it off, he had short spiky blue hair. *Why didn't I see him yesterday after school?* I thought to myself.

He scanned the bus as he walked down the aisle. I assumed he was looking for someone he could talk to. My heart dropped. I vowed to myself, right then and there, that we would be together.

I'd had crushes on celebrities and some of my classmates before, but I'd never had a feeling like this. I'd never even kissed a boy. Besides, all of the boys at my middle school had never shown any interest in me.

He stopped two seats in front of me and I couldn't take my eyes off him.

A few stops later, I was surprised to see Nancy get on the bus. Naturally, she took a seat next to me. The high school was on the outskirts of town, so it was great to find that Nancy was assigned to my bus. Even so, I was entranced by that boy.

I must have been ignoring Nancy because she started shaking my shoulders. 'Chica, what's got into you?' she asked, confused.

Whispering, I said, 'See that boy up there. The one with the blue hair? I think I'm in love.'

She peeked up, looking for him.

'Oh him. Yeah, I saw him in the halls yesterday.'

'Really? Where?' I asked, excited.

Laughing she said, 'I don't know. I just remember his hair.'

When the bus stopped at school, I wanted to follow him. Nancy had other plans though, and dragged me to the cafeteria.

'But. But. I want to see him.' I stammered, looking over my shoulder, watching him disappear into the crowd.

Letting go of my arm, she said, 'Fine. Go talk to him.'

Grabbing her arm back, I said, 'Oh God no! I'm not going to make a fool of myself.'

We laughed, and headed towards the cafe, in the opposite direction of the boy. In between each period I searched the masses of kids for blue hair. I couldn't see him anywhere. After school I waited anxiously in my seat for him to get on the bus. Nancy sat next to me.

'Still waiting for him?' she teased.

'I don't know what it is about him. I've had crushes before, but this. This is something completely different,' I said, swooning.

'I've never seen you like this. It's weird,' she giggled.

When the bus was full, the driver shut the doors and we took off. But he wasn't onboard! I looked out the window and scanned the crowd for him, but had no luck.

Nancy's stop was first. After we dropped her and some elementary kids off, the bus went to the middle school to pick up the sixth to eighth graders. The new girl I'd seen in the morning got on the bus. She looked around, and seemed disappointed. She sat in the seat just behind the driver and quizzed him.

'Do you know where my brother is?'

The driver shrugged her shoulders, and then proceeded to yell at some kids in the back who were standing on the seats. When I got home, I was already living for the next day. I might get to see him again. My crush had transported me away from thinking about my discovery; I didn't have to think now about how to deal with the realisation that my mom was a hoarder.

• • •

When I got up, I made sure my hair and make-up were perfect. I'd never dated before, and I wasn't sure how to start, but I knew I wanted to be with him. At least find out his name.

I got on the bus and waited until we got to his street. I peeked over the seat, hoping I would see him standing in his driveway. I was disappointed when I saw his sister standing there, alone. Suddenly their front door swung open, and he ran outside. This time his hair wasn't spiked, it just fell wherever. It looked funny.

He passed me in the aisle. I wanted to look over my shoulder at him, but I couldn't without it being obvious. I waited patiently until Nancy got on the bus. I devised a plan. I was going to sit sideways in the seat while talking to Nancy, and then I could look at him all I wanted. My plan backfired though, and I got yelled at by the driver for facing the wrong way.

When she yelled my name, the boy looked up and we made eye contact. I looked away, nervous.

Well, at least he knows I exist, I thought, smiling to myself.

The rest of my week was spent trying to pick him out of the crowded bus and trying to look at him without him noticing. He caught me a few times, and even smiled at me once. My heart melted. I was upset when the weekend rolled around, because I couldn't get my fix.

Sunday night I started getting a cold. It was nothing serious, but I took some painkillers and went to sleep. When the alarm went off in the morning, I could barely stand. I steadied myself against the dresser, and managed to turn the alarm off.

I slipped on my flip-flops, and made my way to Mom's room, leaning against the wall as I went along. I shook Mom's leg to wake her up. When I tried speaking, nothing came out. She sat up quickly, and asked, 'What's wrong kiddo?'

I pointed to my throat, and shook my head. She rolled her eyes, and said, 'Well, I'll call the school to let them know you're going to miss today. Not a good way to start the new school year. Go grab me the phone.'

It took me a while, but I finally found the phone, and sat at the foot of her bed, avoiding her piss spots. She called, hung up and looked at me, hard.

'Well if you're going to be home all day, you may as well do laundry. My blankets need to be washed,' she ordered.

I took a sip from a bottle of water I had picked up from the kitchen. The moisture felt great, and I managed to speak in a low whisper.

'It hurts so much to breathe. I can't take a full breath, and I'm getting light headed,' I pleaded, between breaths.

Sliding past me, she said, 'You'll be fine. Do laundry, but otherwise, take it easy.'

Do laundry? Did she have any idea how much effort it took to heave her sodden, heavy blankets downstairs? Exhausted, I fell back on my bed.

• • •

A little while later, I woke up. I couldn't breathe. I sat up quickly, fighting to take air in, but nothing happened. I grabbed my water and took a few big swigs. My throat finally started relaxing and I could breathe again. I looked at my alarm clock, and it said it was just past noon.

Sighing, I got up, slipped my shoes on and grabbed my mom's pissy blankets. As they plopped to the ground, the stench hit me. My swollen throat closed up, and the fumes coming off the blankets burned my eyes. I walked into my room, gasping to catch my breath. I finally got my breathing to an even pace and tried to take a deep glug of air. My lungs weren't even half full but they were burning.

I made my way out of my mom's room, dragging the blankets to the upstairs door. There was so much crap on the stairs that I had to throw the blankets to the landing at the bottom, instead of letting them tumble down. The blankets were so heavy with urine, that when they landed, the windows shook.

The windows vibrated for a few seconds before quieting down. As I made my way down the stairs, piss drained from the mass of blankets. A pool formed until it got so big, it started trickling down the stairs to the laundry room. When I walked past the blankets, my flip-flops failed me – the pool of piss was so deep that my foot was half covered. I shuddered, and kept going.

I pulled the blankets into the laundry room and started coughing. I could feel my face getting red and hot. I was coughing so much I couldn't catch my breath. My knees gave out, and I fell to the ground. I started seeing stars and, just when I thought I was about to pass out, I managed to take a breath.

I was gasping. I took my hand away from my mouth and was horrified to see blood spattered across my palm. I panicked and ran upstairs, but I stopped after climbing just a few steps. I was so out of breath and it felt like someone was stabbing me in the lungs. I had to take a few breaks, but I finally made it upstairs, wheezing. I grabbed the phone, and called Mom at her work.

'Hi, you've reached the kitchen. How may I help you?' her co-worker, Miranda, asked.

'Can I talk to my mom?' I rasped.

'Britney?'

'Yeah,' I squeaked out.

'You know it's lunch and your mom's on the grill right now. She can't really leave,' she explained apologetically.

'I'm coughing up blood,' I spluttered.

I heard a gulp. 'Give me a sec. I'll get your mom.'

A few moments later, Mom picked up the phone.

'What's going on? Miranda said you're coughing up blood.'

'Yeah. I'm scared. I don't know what's going on,' I said, starting to whimper.

'Just calm down. I can't leave work right now. Miranda is taking over the grill for me, but it's lunch rush, so I can't be gone long. Let me call Barbra. I know she's coming in in a little bit. I'll see if she can pick you up on the way in,' she said, trying to help and find a solution.

'Please do it quickly,' I said.

'I'll call you back in a little bit. Okay?'

'Okay bye,' I said, before hanging up.

A few minutes later, the phone rang. I answered.

'Mom?'

'Barbra will pick you up in less than thirty minutes. Get ready to go, and keep an eye out for her. I don't want her going up to the house,' she warned.

I waited by the door, keeping an eye out for Barbra. When she pulled up, I slipped out the front door so she wouldn't have a chance to see inside. The walk to the car was so tiring, I was out of breath when I sat down. Between coughs, I said, 'Thank you for getting me.'

'No problem, hon,' she said, backing out of the driveway.

• • •

We got to the hospital where my mom was waiting for me with a wheelchair.

'Oh my God. You look terrible,' she said, pushing me towards the ER.

I coughed the entire way, getting some nasty looks from other hospital staff. When we got to the ER, I was rushed immediately into the back. I'd never been to the Emergency Room before. I was so scared. But the nurses who were working on me were talking over my head to my mom about what was on the menu for the rest of the week. It helped me relax.

Sliding a breathing mask over my face, the nurse said, 'This is oxygen and albuterol. You're probably going to feel funny for a minute, but you need to take as many deep breaths as you can muster. Okay?'

Looking over the mask, I nodded my head. She flipped the switch, turning on the oxygen. I took a deep breath. It felt good, but it hurt so much that I vomited into the mask. Annoyed, the nurse turned off the oxygen and got me set up with another breathing mask.

'If you're going to throw up this time, take the mask off and throw up in here,' she said, placing a waste bin next to my bed.

After an hour on the machine, my breathing didn't get a whole lot better. The ER staff helped me into a wheelchair, and took me away to get a CT scan. It was nerve-racking to be in the tube, hearing it hum around me. The nurses told me to lie still, but I couldn't breathe while I was on my back and kept coughing.

I saw two technicians through the observation window point to me. One of them made an unpleasant face, and then shook her head. It made me super nervous.

'All right, we'll get you back on the oxygen,' one of them said, coming out of the room. She helped me off the CT machine and into the wheelchair.

'What's wrong with me?' I asked her on the ride back to the ER.

Patting my shoulder, she said, 'You'll be okay. I can't tell you what I saw because we have to get a second opinion, but you'll know shortly.'

Well, that was reassuring. I tried not to let my mind race ahead to the wrong conclusion.

As I was wheeled into my room, my mom was preoccupied, joking with some of the staff. I laid back down, put my mask on and fell asleep. I dreamt of the boy down the road. I was really bummed that I didn't get to see him today.

I don't know how long I was out, but the next thing I knew, Mom woke me up, and someone else was in the room.

'Hi Britney, how do you feel?' a doctor asked nicely.

Sitting up I said, 'Good. I can breathe a lot better, but it still hurts.'

He flicked through some papers he had in his hands.

'Looking at your charts, you've got bacterial bronchitis. That means you've got an infection, and you need to take it easy for a few days. No school. I've written down some medicine you need to take, but otherwise you should be good to go home.'

'Bronchitis? But how did I get that?' I asked. I was nervous and looked at my mom for confirmation that everything was going to be all right. Instead, she was busy scraping the gook out from underneath her fingernails.

'Well, it could be caused by a number of things. If you're not used to cigarette smoke, that could have bothered your lungs. Dust, mould, mildew are other culprits,' he explained.

That filthy house is why I have bronchitis.

I pulled the blankets back and climbed out of the bed. I felt much better than I did earlier, but my lungs were still on fire. Mom helped me to the car and she carried my prescriptions. I didn't even wait to get home to take my pills. Sitting in the passenger seat, I popped them in my mouth, one at a time and swallowed them with cranberry juice.

When we pulled up at our trash-filled house, I had to steady my head. The medicine had made me feel funny. As I climbed the front steps, I was out of breath. I felt bad because I was taking so long and Mom was behind me, unable to pass. As soon as I opened the door, the smell of the house hit me like a brick wall, making my lungs seize.

I pulled out the inhaler the doctor had prescribed me and took two, long puffs. I could breathe a bit better, but all of the mould in the house – in the kitchen, on the damp clothes, on all the takeaway containers – made it hard to take in air. To help loosen my lungs, I took a hot shower. I had to wait ages for the hot water to come through because our plumbing was starting to go wrong.

Letting the water cascade down my body, I thought about how I wasn't going to be able to see the boy from the bus for a while. When I stepped out of the shower, I saw the piles of rubbish and dirty clothes that were never going to be washed. The realisation that I was going to have to stay in the house that made me ill loomed over me. *It's not fair: why do I have to live like this?*

I dried my body off, and got in my pyjamas. As I drifted to sleep, my friends' faces flashed through my mind. I was going to miss them over the next couple of days. Then the face of the boy from the bus came into my head. I was going to miss seeing him the most.

I didn't know whom this boy really was, but he'd become a little nugget of hope for me – something to keep me going. A tear ran down my cheek as I realised his face was already fading from my mind.

I drifted off to sleep.

CHAPTER 13

Nancy had learnt that the boy with the blue hair was in the year above us, and also that he had left our school for another one nearby – that's why I never saw him around the building. He still used my bus though. I would see him make his way to where Nancy and I were slouched on our way home and my heart would began to race.

'Just talk to him,' Nancy would say, poking my side.

'But I don't know what to say,' I'd reply, watching him intently.

• • •

I started on my homework as soon as I got home. Now that I was in high school, I had a lot more homework I had to focus on instead of chores. My mom sort of understood, but she still got mad at times. And I was still doing all the laundry.

When Mom got home from work one day, I was still working on my studies.

'Can you sit on the stool? I want the couch.' she pointed.

'I guess, but I've still got quite a bit left to do.'

'You know what? Fuck it, just sit there. I'll watch TV in my room,' she said, suddenly furious at me.

I shrugged, and continued working on my homework. I noticed that she didn't move though. She just stood there, eyeballing me.

'Well?' she said, hands on her hips.

'Well what?' I asked, solving a math problem.

'Aren't you going to move?' she asked, annoyed.

Not looking up, I said, 'Didn't you just say you were going to your room?'

'Well, I want to watch TV out here. Move!' She stepped in front of me.

'Whatever,' I mumbled, gathering my stuff so I could sit on my stool.

Before Mom sat down, she took off her shirt, and threw it in front of the upstairs door. She then took off her trousers and her underwear, and left them by her feet. She hadn't even sat down yet and I could smell her. A combination of sweat, unwashed privates and hospital food filled the air. I quickly tucked my nose in the collar of my shirt so I didn't have to smell it anymore.

Balancing my textbook, homework, pencil and

calculator on my knees, I continued my studies. After a while, my legs and bum turned numb. My stool was so low to the ground it was almost like I was squatting. I managed to finish my homework and stretched my legs. I wished I could pace the hallway, but I didn't want to worry about tripping over something or squeezing past the towering piles of trash.

• • •

As I waited for the bus the next morning, I thought to myself, *You've got to talk to him today. Invite him to sit with you.*

The moment I stepped on the bus, I was nervous. It was going to be a while before he got on, but that anticipation was making it worse. We finally turned onto his road, and I could see him and his sister waiting.

When he got on, he sat with one of the kids who had always been mean to me. I used that as my cue to chat to him. I scooted over and leaned in.

'Hey, you really don't want to sit with him. Here, take a seat,' I said patting the seat next to me.

He looked at me and then back at the kid he was going to sit with, and finally sat next to me. My heart was beating so fast I could hear it in my ears. *Oh my God, what do I do next?* I thought.

With a big smile on his face, he extended his hand out.

'Hey, I'm Adam.'

I reached out and shook his hand. The moment our hands touched I felt a warm tingle. *I wonder if he feels it too?*

Smiling back, I said, 'I'm Britney. So did you just move to the area?'

'Yeah, I just moved midway through the summer. How about you? Have you been here long?' he asked, interested.

'Yes, I've lived here my entire life,' I laughed. If only he knew how much I wished I was starting my life over.

We talked for the entire bus ride. When Nancy got on, she gave me a big knowing smile and a thumbs up when she saw Adam and I were sitting with each other. She sat in the seat in front of us. They introduced themselves, and seemed to get along. Then we all got off the bus, and Nancy and I left Adam so he could catch his other bus to school.

Walking away, Nancy whispered, 'What was it about today that made you talk to him?'

'I don't know. I just wanted to,' I said. I was walking on cloud nine, I felt invincible.

After school Nancy and I sat together. When

Adam got on the bus, he sat in front of us, and we all shared stories about our day. When Nancy got off, he quickly got up and sat with me. I could hear my heart beating in my ears again.

• • •

For months we sat next to each other, every day. Nancy even stopped sitting with me on the way back from school so Adam could. We became instant friends, and he even joined the same after-school groups as me so we could hang out more. I felt like I could trust him, that I could say anything and he wouldn't judge me for it.

Mom was getting annoyed hearing about Adam all the time. I would tell her almost everything he told me. I told her how much I liked him, and how badly I wanted to be with him. I guess somewhere I thought she might like me more if she knew a boy liked me.

On our way back from school one day, Adam nervously asked the question I had been dreading. 'Can I come over to yours sometime, and hang out?'

Looking down at my feet, I swallowed hard. I'd never had this conversation with anyone before. Not even properly with Nancy. I had no choice though – I had to tell him the truth, I couldn't hold him at arm's length forever.

'I've never told anybody this, but ...' I paused.

Leaning in he said, 'But?'

I made eye contact with him. His eyes were a gorgeous light blue that I could get lost in. Struggling for words, I told him the truth: 'My mom's a hoarder, it's really bad. I don't want anybody, especially you, to see it.'

He smiled kindly, and took my hand.

'I completely understand. Before I moved in with my mom, I lived in a hoarder's house too. My stepmom was really bad. She hoarded furniture. What does your mom hoard?' he asked.

This was fate. I couldn't believe the guy I really liked had suffered the same as me. I let out a sigh of relief. I was still nervous though, because hoarding trash was much worse than hoarding furniture.

'She doesn't throw away trash because she feels it's still useful. She holds onto newspapers, old clothes, bottles, food. And she's kinda lazy,' I added, embarrassed.

He tightened his grip on my hand, and squeezed it.

'That sucks, I'm sorry to hear that. If you don't want me coming over, then do you want to come to my place instead?'

Perking up, I said, 'I'd love to. But I have to ask my mom first.'

Smiling, he grabbed a pen, and wrote his number on the back of my hand.

'If your mom wants to talk to my parents, here is the house phone. How does this Friday sound?'

'Oh, that's perfect,' I yelped, as we pulled up to my house. 'Friday sounds great. I'll have my mom call when she gets home from work. Bye.'

'Bye,' he said, waving.

Mom was hesitant about me going over to Adam's. She wasn't happy that her little girl was going to hang out with a boy, but she felt better after she called his mom and dad, and let the bus driver know my plans.

• • •

Friday came around quickly and Adam, his sister and I walked into their house together. We were greeted by two big dogs, a blonde and a black one. They were barking and seemed angry, and they made me super nervous. I stood in the doorway until his mom ushered them into her living room.

Then Adam's mom walked up to me and gave me a hug.

'Sorry, they're not mean, they just like talking. I'm Lisa, nice to meet you.'

She let go and I followed her into the living room. Sitting down, I said, 'It's no problem, it's just the bark that gets me. I'm Britney, by the way.'

225

After the awkward introductions, Adam and I went upstairs to hang out in his bedroom. On our way, his mom reminded us to keep the door open. He had held my hand once, but apart than that, we hadn't done anything. Adam's face turned red with embarrassment.

'Whatever Mom,' he yelled.

We listened to music, ate pizza and talked a lot more. There was so much electricity between us in the room it almost felt uncomfortable.

Adam looked straight into my eyes and pulled my hand towards him. He sandwiched my palm between his hands, and the warmth spread up my arms and covered my body like a blanket. Butterflies flew around in my stomach. *Is this the part when he is supposed to kiss me?* I felt so nervous; I had no idea how to kiss.

Just as Adam was leaning in, I heard the doorbell go.

'That's my mom. I have to go. Bye,' I said, scrambling to my feet.

'Bye, see you on Monday,' Adam grinned. He waved me off.

• • •

A few weeks later, there was a Valentine's dance was coming up. Most of my high school was going, and local bands were playing. I wasn't sure if Adam was going, let alone if he would invite me. I really wanted him to, but after we held hands, nothing else had happened. We had hung out a lot, smoked weed, listened to music and talked, but that was it.

The morning of the day before the dance, Adam was acting weird. He wasn't talking to me, and wouldn't even look at me. When we got off the bus, we went to our usual spot, to wait for his bus to take him to school.

Standing there awkwardly, Adam faced me, grabbed my hands, and asked, 'Do you want to go to the dance with me tomorrow?'

I bit my lip as I smiled.

'Of course. I was wondering if you were going to ask,' I grinned.

Letting out a sigh of relief, he said, 'Oh, thank God. I already asked my mom, and she'll drive us there and she'll give you a ride home.'

'That's awesome. I can't wait,' I said, squeezing his hands.

'That's my bus. I have to go.'

He kissed me on the cheek and walked off.

I put the palm of my hand to my cheek, where he had just kissed me. I could feel the heat from where his lips had touched me. The rest of the day was a daze. I was so nervous, yet excited for the next day. When Adam sat next to me after school he was really cool and never mentioned the brief kiss. We talked like normal.

My mom got home, and before she was up the stairs, I excitedly told her my news.

'I don't need a ride to the dance tomorrow. Adam's mom is going to give me a ride there and back.'

Mom turned to me. Her eyes narrowed and her forehead crumpled into a deep scowl.

'So is it a date?' she asked, annoyed.

I was upset with her reaction. *Why can't she be happy for me?*

'I don't know. Maybe.'

She stared at me for a long minute without saying a word. I was back on tenterhooks, waiting for either her explosion or for her to say something nice.

She didn't say anything at all. Mom turned and walked off, kicking some trash out the way as she went.

Adam's mom picked me up a few hours before the dance so we could get something to eat. As we were walking up to the gym hall where the dance was being held, Adam grabbed my hand. My stomach fluttered. *Finally, all the other girls at school will see that I can have a boyfriend too. I'm not so different after all.*

We spent the night dancing with my friends, who thankfully liked Adam, and Adam liked them. A slow song came on and everyone started splitting into couples. Adam took one of my hands, put the other on his waist, and we started dancing. I put my head on his chest and we rocked back and forth, just like they do in the movies.

Halfway through the song, I looked up at him. His eyes were so kind. He had got rid of his blue spikes and his blonde hair was a few inches long. I don't know what compelled me to do it, but I got up on my tippy toes and kissed him, smack on the lips. He kissed me back – gently grabbing the back of my head as he did so. The music stopped. The crowd left. It was just him and me, floating.

When we stopped kissing we realised a different song was now playing, which was fast and upbeat. My friends were all whispering, saying things like, 'They finally kissed. That took a while.' The rest of the night was spent dodging teachers and chaperones, so we could make out.

• • •

The rest of the school year was spent wrapped up in Adam's arms, kissing on his bed.

'You should sneak over. You know, in the middle of the night,' he suggested one evening in June.

'What? You're kidding right?' I said, shocked.

He started whispering so his parents couldn't hear.

'No. That door goes to our back yard,' he pointed, cheekily.

He had a door on the side of his room. I stared at it and asked, 'When?'

'Why not tonight?' he said, smiling.

I was nervous – I had never done anything like that before.

'Sure. Do I just come in? Do you want me to knock?'

'Don't knock. That will wake the dogs up. Just come in quietly. I'll know it's you,' he said, stroking my cheek.

• • •

That night, I set an alarm on my cellphone for midnight. I tucked it under my pillow so it would muffle the alarm enough for Mom not to hear it. Luckily, her weight made her a heavy sleeper. I was so nervous that I never actually went to sleep. I waited and waited for the alarm to go off so I could leave. My mom started snoring at around 11 p.m., and was still hammering away when it was time to go.

I quickly turned off the alarm, and made my bed so it looked like I was sleeping in it. Holding my breath, I tiptoed past my mom's room. I slowly slid the chain off the upstairs lock, trying my best not to make the metal squeal.

The upstairs door always boomed loudly, like thunder, when it was opened. It took ten minutes, but I eventually managed to open the door without any noise. The next challenge was trying to go down the stairwell which echoed. Each step moaned with the slightest pressure, and the stairwell amplified it. I slowly crept down, skipping fours steps at a time, to avoid extra noise. I stopped every now and again to listen for my mom's snores. They kept coming, so I kept descending.

I finally made it to the platform at the bottom of the stairs. I was sweating from trying so hard to be quiet and I was super nervous. I knew there was no way I was going to be able to open the front door, so I cleared the table in front of the window in the laundry room and scrambled on top of it. I slowly opened the window, which thankfully didn't make any noise.

Holding my breath so I could listen for my mom's snoring, I waited. After a few seconds, she let out a loud snore. I breathed out, and slid out the window.

I ran down the porch to the post where my bike was locked. I got on and peddled as fast as I could until I was sure the trees masked me. I then slowed down, because I didn't want to be sweaty when I showed up to Adam's place.

• • •

I parked my bike behind the empty house next door, and quietly opened the gate to his back yard. Standing right outside his bedroom, I reached out my hand onto the doorknob. I checked my phone for the time. It was already 1 a.m., I was shocked it took me an hour to sneak out and ride my bike less than a mile.

I took a deep breath and opened the door, slowly. Adam sat up and rolled over to make room on the bed for me. I slid into bed with him. He kissed my cheek and stroked my hair as we cuddled.

We quietly whispered to each other, giggling, softly. Adam was in his boxers, I was in my bra and panties. We lay, entangled. Adam grabbed me by my waist, and pulled me close to him. He nuzzled my neck and then put his lips very close to my ear.

'Britney. I think I'm in love. I love you,' he whispered.

He dropped his head to my shoulder and waited for my response.

I took a deep breath and said it: 'I've wanted to tell you that for a few weeks now. I love you too.' I wrapped my arms around his neck and gave him a big kiss. We fell back with a soft thud, and made out for what seemed like forever.

It was 5.30 a.m. and the two of us were fighting off sleep. I couldn't set an alarm because that would wake his parents up, but I couldn't risk falling asleep. Adam kept readjusting himself and finally whispered, 'My boxers keep riding up.'

I didn't say anything, we just lay there. We had only been together for four months, and we'd only known each other for eight. Not to mention, both of us were fourteen and still virgins.

I checked the time, and had fifteen minutes before it was 6 a.m. Suddenly Adam started squirming around, kicking his legs. He stopped, and threw something across his room. My heart quickened. *Did he just take off his boxers?* I thought, as I cuddled him. I got very close so I could reach down and feel if he had taken them off.

As my hand slid down his body, it touched his hard penis. He reached over, and slid my panties off. It took a minute of trying, but it finally happened. It hurt, but it was perfect, and when we were done, we cuddled.

Suddenly, I was aware of the time. It was 6.15., fifteen minutes after the time I needed to leave. I quickly got dressed, gave Adam a kiss and bolted out of the door. I raced home, hoping my mom was still asleep. I put my bike away, and climbed back in the window. I strained to hear her snores and was relieved when I heard one.

Now that I knew my mom wouldn't catch me, I felt free. I walked upstairs, this time not caring about the noise. *I'll just tell Mom that I wanted to watch the news.*

Mom didn't wake up as I climbed the creaky stairs, or even when I opened up the thunderous door. I shut it behind me, locked it and climbed into my bed. I lay there thinking about my first time. Every so often I caught myself smiling as I relived the moment. I hugged my chest imagining Adam was with me in my bed.

Not for one moment did I think about the trash. I didn't think about the takeaway containers and soda bottles blocking my doorway. I didn't hear the scratching of the mice around my bed. All I could think about was when I would escape again. I'd found a trapdoor out of this place.

• • •

By the time it was the summer holidays, I had perfected the art of sneaking out. Six nights of the week I was at Adam's house by 12.30 a.m. We would have sex and just talk for hours. I always got back around 6 a.m. Only once was my mom awake upstairs. I just sat in the living room, watching TV, quietly, until I heard her telltale snore start up again.

During the holidays I was getting up later and later the following day, as I was trying to catch up on my sleep.

It was already 2 p.m. by the time I woke up one afternoon. I heated up the pork chops and mashed potatoes Mom had brought home from work the day before, and ate while watching trash TV.

Someone knocked loudly on the door, making me jump and drop my food. I brushed the mashed potatoes off my legs, and went down to see who it could be. *Oh my God, it's Adam.* I opened the front door, stepped out and quickly pulled it to, so he didn't see what lay behind. He wrapped his arms around me and hugged me tight.

'I'm horny,' he said, smiling.

'Me too. But where?' I panicked.

Adam looked baffled, like I had said something strange.

'Here of course. Your mom isn't coming home until six, right?'

'Yeah, but it's a mess. I don't really want you seeing it.' I cringed, looking back at the house.

He kissed my forehead and sat down on the patio step.

'I understand. I don't want to make you uncomfortable.'

'Can you give me a few minutes? Then I'll come get you,' I said, walking towards the front door.

'No problem. So, does this mean we get sexy times?' he asked, raising his eyebrow.

Laughing, I said, 'Yes, sexy times. Just a few minutes.'

I went to the laundry room and grabbed as many old sheets as I could carry from a pile that hadn't been touched in years. They smelled musty, but they didn't have any holes, and the stains weren't too bad.

I ran upstairs, and picked up some thumbtacks from my bookshelf. I carefully tacked the sheets over the doorways to the kitchen, the living room and the bathroom. I then kicked as much of the dirty laundry and trash as I could into the bathroom, trying to make some room to walk.

I didn't have enough sheets to cover my mom's door, so I kicked all of the shit in front of her door to the side, and yanked the door until it became unstuck. Her door still didn't have a doorknob, so I hooked my fingers into the hole where it had once been and tried to yank it shut the rest of the way. The last pull shut the door completely, but my finger slipped, and I got a splinter. I kicked more garbage to the sides of the hallway in anger.

I looked down the hall, it was a disgusting mess, but luckily my sheets would stop Adam from seeing the rest of the house. *He'll sure as hell smell it though*, I thought, as I made my way downstairs.

I opened the door, and nervously motioned for Adam to come in. I grabbed his hand and led him up the stairwell. I took a deep breath and shoved the upstairs door open. We were greeted with my Lion King sheets from when I was seven years old and a piss-stained flowery sheet. As I was shutting the door, Adam pulled at the edge of the sheet, to sneak a look into the living room.

I quickly grabbed his hand, and yanked him down the hallway.

'Please don't,' I begged, stepping over a trash bag. I was moving quickly so we could get to my room and he wouldn't see the mess anymore.

Finally, we got there.

'Wow, this wasn't what I was expecting,' Adam

exclaimed when we stepped inside my bedroom.

My room was my sanctuary. Apart from the tiny clearing of space around my stool in the living room, this was the only clean area in the house. I couldn't control how my mom lived, but there was no way I was going to be like her. The first thing you saw was my desk in the corner, in front the closet. I had blockaded the closet years ago, when a family of sparrows had burrowed through the wall, into my room. On the desk there were stacks of books.

Next to the desk, blocking one of my windows, was a wicker bookshelf. It was packed with my favourite books, and books I had yet to read. My dressing table was in the middle of my room, with its back towards my bed. It held trophies from kung fu, soccer, softball, tennis, swimming and all of the other sports I played. It also had all of my school work from previous years, neatly organised by year and subject, and my clothes were neatly folded inside the dresser draws.

I made my bed like a fortress. All four sides of it were up against some sort of wall, and there was a few feet of space by my head for me to hop in and out of bed. My bed protected me from the trash and the vermin. I had mounted a full length mirror at the foot of the bed, so I could do my make-up and check out what I was wearing.

'What were you expecting?' I asked.

Sitting in the opening to my bed he said, 'Honestly? I thought it was going to be messy, but I like it.'

I slid past Adam, and sat on my bed.

'It used to be, but I couldn't stand it. So one day I threw everything that wasn't important away. Now I have this.'

I grabbed Adam from behind, and pulled him down next to me on the bed. I gently kissed him and slipped off his shirt. He sat up, and started to inch my shirt off. Suddenly, he stopped, and laughed.

'What's wrong? What did I do?' I asked, self-conscious. I tugged my shirt back, and hid my belly with my blanket.

This was the first time Adam had seen me naked, in daylight. Every other time we'd had sex, it had been in the middle of the night.

Pulling the blanket away from me, he said, 'Nothing. I just saw the mirror and thought about how awesome it would be to watch us have sex. Now come here.'

He slipped my shirt off, pushed me back and quickly pulled my shorts and underwear off. Adam paused, and looked at me with a smile on his face. 'You know? You're beautiful.'

He struggled out of his shorts, and we started having sex.

• • •

Later, he rolled off to the edge of the bed, both of us breathing heavily. I turned to my side and snuggled close to him, and we lay still for a few minutes.

'Babe?' he asked, squeezing my shoulder gently.

'What's up?' I said, propping myself up on my elbow.

'Please don't get upset, but would you mind if we went back outside?'

He paused, then looked at me kindly. 'Your house smells,' he said simply, with an empathetic look on his face.

My heart sank. I was having such a good time with him, but no matter how much I tried to hide the mess, I couldn't hide the smell.

'Sure,' I said, defeated.

I got up, and started putting my clothes on. I'd just slid my shorts on, when Adam grabbed my hips, and sat me on his lap.

'Babe, I don't think any less of you, please know that. It's not your fault. But you have to admit, your house smells. You know I love you, right?' he said, kissing my shoulder.

I got up and kissed him on the lips. 'Thank you for understanding.'

When we started walking down the hallway Adam paused and asked if he could use my bathroom. I looked at him like he was insane.

'Do you just have to pee?'

'Yeah, that's all,' he said, giving me a weird look.

'Then no, you can pee in the back yard,' I said, shaking my head.

When we passed my mom's room, a ray of light shone through the doorknob hole. It was very noticeable because our hallway didn't have any light.

'What's this?' Adam asked.

Before I knew what he was talking about, he was already peering through the hole. He slowly put his hand to his mouth.

There were no sheets on Mom's bed so the 'crater' dissolved from Mom's urine was very obvious. It was brown and soggy. Filthy pillows were strewn across the mattress. The trash was so bad now it was level with the bed. There were dozens of empty soda bottles Mom had picked up from the drive-through, mixed in with polystyrene burger boxes, sweet wrappings. The smell of old food remains smelt like rotting flesh.

Adam gagged and covered his mouth and nose. He looked horrified, and grabbed my hand.

'I'm so, so sorry. I wish I'd never seen that. I can't believe you have to live like this,' he gasped with sad eyes.

We went outside, and hung out on the trampoline in the garden. Before Adam left, he grabbed both of my hands and said, 'I promise, one day I will rescue you. You will never have to see this God awful place ever again. I don't know when, I don't know how. But I will. I love you so much.'

He kissed me on the forehead and left. As I watched Adam until he disappeared down the road, a feeling of deep sadness washed over me. *That's easy for you to say Adam.*

I wanted to believe him, but it seemed like an unbelievable fairy tale ending. I could never even trust what mood my mom would be in when she got home from work, so how could I really trust anyone?

CHAPTER 14

'Britney, I need your help. Come here,' my mom yelled from her room.

I got up, and headed over to her. I heard her moving things, and making all sorts of noise. When I walked around the corner, she had pulled her mattress off her bed.

'What are you doing?' I asked, gagging from the smell.

'I'm getting a new mattress tonight, and I need this one out of here. Grab that end and help me get it outside,' she ordered, pointing to the end nearest me. It was brown and soggy. You just needed to press it lightly, and piss would seep to the surface.

Shaking my head, I said, 'I'm not touching that. It's disgusting.'

'The fuck you aren't. Do you want to see Adam tonight?' she threatened me.

'Fine,' I gave in. I grabbed a couple of grocery bags that were crumpled at my feet to make sure my hands didn't touch the bed. I grabbed the mattress, dragging it with all of my might. I wanted to be done quickly, so I didn't wait for my mom to get ready, I just pulled.

'Whoa, slow down,' she said, almost falling forwards.

'No, I'm not going to touch this vile thing any longer than I have to,' I said, yanking it through the hallway. The mattress bent around the door frame, and with one last yank, it came free, spraying me with old musty piss.

I spat the piss out of my mouth and shouted, 'God fucking damn it!'

'Watch your mouth,' Mom said, peeking around the piss-stained mattress.

'It's fucking disgusting. I just got your pee in my fucking mouth!' I yelled, as I wiped my face with my arms.

Mom knew she had lost the battle. She stopped arguing and helped me shove the mattress past the upstairs door and into the kitchen. She opened the door, and I guided the mattress into the stairwell. I moved the mattress against the wall, and kicked it down the stairs. We kept the front door open, so when it landed, it bounced outside, landing with a wet thud.

'So are we dragging it to the pit?' I asked, as I went down the stairs.

'I don't think so. The grass is too tall in the back yard to drag it, and the pit is getting pretty full.'

'So, what are we going to do with it?'

She picked up a corner of the mattress, and dragged it to the side of the porch.

'I guess it's good here for now.'

Looking at her with bewilderment, I said, 'Do you realise how white trash that looks? School is starting soon, and everyone on the bus is going to see we have an old dirty mattress on our porch.'

'Oh it's not that bad. It's landed the good side up. And nobody is paying attention to our house anyway,' Mom shrugged me off.

And so the foul mattress stayed where it was.

• • •

School started, and soon I was exhausted. I had to leave Adam's at 5 a.m. instead of 6, to ensure I would be home before my alarm went off. *I'll just sleep in class*, I thought one morning, as I was putting on my make-up.

I got on the bus and fell asleep as soon as I sat down. The next thing I knew, Adam was shaking me awake.

'Hey, sleepy head,' he said, grabbing my hand.

'I'm so tired – we might just do Fridays and Saturdays,' I said, resting my head on his shoulder.

'Yeah, I'm pooped. That sounds good.' He kissed the back of my hand.

• • •

I continued sneaking to Adam's house at weekends until it got too cold to cycle there at night. A month and a half into my sophomore year, I got bronchitis again. It felt as painful as the last time. I was coughing blood and I felt like my chest was on fire. We went to the ER to get more medication, but the doctors never questioned why I had breathing problems for the second time in just over a year.

After the third time of getting bronchitis, I stayed at my grandparents' house until I got better. I was so surprised that Mom had organised this, but so relieved. They lived about twenty minutes away and it felt like another world. It was awesome, I got to play video games, eat home-cooked meals and I got better a hell of a lot quicker than if I had gone back to my mouldy dirty home. I didn't get to see Adam for a week. He'd call every day after school, and we'd talk for hours, until my grandma said it was time for dinner.

My grandparents never talked about the reason I was getting sick all the time. At the time, I thought they didn't realise what the problem was but, looking back, they *must* have known. Aged fifteen, I felt that they didn't really want to talk about Mom's hoarding and I never felt able to raise the subject either. It was like Mom was the elephant in the room.

• • •

After I had finally recovered, I came home from school one day and noticed my mom's room looked brighter than usual. I peeked in, and saw that there was a hole in her ceiling that led to an even bigger hole in our roof. Rain was falling through. I rang Mom, afraid I'd get sick again.

'You're lying. You have to be,' she said in disbelief.

'No, I'm serious. Take a look when you get home. The rain has collapsed part of the ceiling,' I said, looking through the hole.

'Well get a couple of buckets, and put them under the hole to collect rain. If all of that shit in my room gets wet it's going to get really mouldy,' she said in a whisper, so no one at work could hear.

'Yeah, I'll get it done,' I said, hanging up.

I collected all of the buckets I could find, and shoved piles of rubbish out of the way so I could get the buckets under the hole. I had to dig small holes and plant the buckets in the rubbish. The buckets caught some of the rain, but the hole was so big, rain still spewed everywhere.

Mom got home from work, and inspected the hole. It was about the size of a soccerball and the wood had rotted away. The rain must have soaked the drywall on the ceiling until a big chunk had finally fallen in. My mom's solution was to stick an umbrella through the hole and open it, shielding the hole, leaving the handle inside. We planted the handle next to a support beam, hoping it wouldn't come loose. It stopped rain from directly falling in, but that rain trickled down the sides of the umbrella, and ended up inside the house anyway. It only took one good storm to blow the umbrella out of the hole, and Mom didn't bother putting another one up.

Mom got a quote over the phone for the roof, but she was convinced that she could get it done cheaper elsewhere. She kept ringing round, until she finally found someone cheap enough. I could tell she was uncomfortable with the idea of a stranger visiting our house though. She was shouting and kicking trash around with her bare toes. She ordered me to get to work on filling bags. I did as I was told because I wanted the roof to be fixed. I didn't want to get sick again.

The guy came around in the morning and there was no disguising the look of disgust on his face. Mom led him up to the bedroom and I trailed behind. I watched the workman's eyes as he kept looking back over his shoulder, as if expecting a monster to jump out from the mess. He barely inspected the hole in the roof. I'm sure he had made up his mind before he took two steps through our house.

'I'm sorry, this is too big a job for me to take on,' he declined.

'Well thanks for wasting my time,' Mom snapped.

He seemed like a nice guy and I cringed with embarrassment. He flashed me a look just as he was leaving. I recognised it well – it was a look of pity. That familiar sinking feeling rose in my belly because I knew what was in store.

After that, just as I predicted, Mom stopped looking for someone to fix the roof. She seemed to stop caring. After a few days of rain we emptied the buckets of water out the window, and put them back, until it rained again. The rubbish below the buckets turned soggy, and the years of trash started compacting.

I dreaded emptying the buckets. The water was brown and had bugs and twigs floating in it. It smelled like death because the trash underneath was getting mouldy. I bought sterile face masks from the store to wear when I emptied the water buckets.

• • •

When another storm hit, all I could hear was the noise of the rain pouring into the buckets in Mom's room. I didn't understand how she slept through it. When the wind picked up, it sprayed her bed with rain water. She just went about her life like it was no big deal.

I was just tucking into the roast chicken and potatoes, which Mom had brought back from the hospital the day before, when she yelled at me.

'When you're done eating could I get your help,' she barked.

'Sure. With what?' I said.

She pulled a plastic bag out of her purse, and showed me some old roof shingles.

'I picked these up from the side of the house last night. I think they're the ones from the hole. We're going to use spray insulating foam to attach them to the roof,' she said proudly.

My jaw dropped.

'You mean we're not going to get it fixed? How are we even going to get up to the roof? We have a two story house?'

'No, I'm not going to have it fixed, smart-ass,' she said. 'I'm planning on moving when you go to college, so why pay several grand for a new roof when I'll only be able to enjoy it for a few years? We will climb into the attic and spray the foam and stick the shingles to it. It'll be easy and watertight if we do it correctly,' she said smiling.

I looked at her like she was crazy. *She was crazy.*

'Whatever.' There was no point in fighting. 'Can I go to Adam's after we're done?'

'That's fine, just wear your helmet on your ride over there,' she said. *Now she's being motherly.*

Of course, because of Mom's size, it was up to me to fix the roof. I had to shimmy across the beams, being careful not to step on the insulation, otherwise I'd fall through the ceiling. I also didn't want to touch the insulation because it made my skin unbearably itchy. The hole was right on the edge of the house, so I had to lie on cardboard, keeping my balance on a narrow beam.

Mom tossed me the spray foam and the shingles, and I pondered over how I was going to fix the hole.

It was now large enough for me to stick my head and one shoulder through. I watched the cars as they passed the house, hoping someone would see me and call the cops.

I filled the hole with foam and placed the wooden tiles over it. I carefully inched the last one into place, creating a perfect seal. I then covered the tiles with more spray foam, trying to make it even more watertight. I went to put another tile on top, but it crumbled in my hands.

'Mom, I need another shingle, this one has disintegrated,' I said, shaking the dust off of me.

'I don't have any more. I grabbed all of the good ones. Just rip some of the cardboard you're lying on, and use that to cover it. Go quick because it's going to dry,' she said, with her hands on her hips.

I ripped off a piece of cardboard, slightly bigger than the hole, and sprayed it with foam. I slapped it up against the roof and held if there for a few minutes. I tugged on the corner to check if it had dried, and the cardboard didn't come loose. I wiggled back to the platform in the attic, admiring my work. Then I did a double take.

You need to get out of this fucking place, I thought, shaking my head.

The patch I did on the roof wasn't watertight, but it did reduce the amount of water coming in. That was until the heavy rains came a month later, and my make-shift roof caved in. I was afraid of getting sick again. The only thing I could be happy for was that it wasn't in my room. I had no idea what my mom's plans were to get it fixed before winter rolled around.

• • •

Halloween came, and Adam asked me to go on a date with him. We were going to go to a haunted house, and then go for dinner. My mom even extended my curfew until midnight as the Boy Scouts were running the haunted house for a homeless charity. It was scary, but Adam held me close, making it fun. They let us go through it a second time for free because of all of the food we had brought for the shelter. Adam's mom waited in the car park for us to finish. After we had been through the house for a second time, I wasn't feeling well. I thought it was because I hadn't eaten.

We went to a local burger restaurant and I felt tremendously better. We then got back to Adam's house, where his parents had a surprise waiting for him. While we were gone, his stepdad, Will, had thrown away Adam's single mattress and replaced it with a queen bed with all of the trimmings. It even had a headboard and footboard.

Adam leapt on his bed and wiggled around on it for a minute.

'You hear that?' he asked, whispering.

'No, what?' I asked, confused.

'It doesn't squeak. We don't have to worry about noise while having sex,' he said, thrusting his hips with a goofy smile on his face.

We lay down on his new bed. I started coughing, and my lungs hurt terribly. The next thing I remembered was Adam, shaking me awake.

'Babe, we called your mom. You passed out and wouldn't wake up,' he said, concerned.

I was so weak that I couldn't get up and breathing was hard. I had to concentrate on every breath. Mom arrived pissed off for having to pick me up. I was supposed to get a ride back from Adam's mom, but they couldn't get me out of the house and into the car. I lay on the bed, while my mom looked down at me, shaking her head.

'I can't fucking believe this. Get up, let's go,' she said, her hands on her hips.

I literally couldn't sit up, let alone get up and go to the car. Adam picked me up, and carried me to the car. He buckled me in and kissed me goodnight. My mom rolled her eyes the entire time, mumbling about how I was being a drama queen. When we pulled up to the house, she left me in the car. It took me forever to get up the stairs, but I was finally in my bed.

I didn't wake up until noon the next day. When I sat on my stool, I started coughing. I felt something pop in my throat, and then I was coughing up blood. I had blood in my hands and on the corners of my mouth. I looked up at Mom, pleading for help.

'Mom, what's happening?'

We rushed to the Urgent Care centre, but they thought I was too extreme a case, so they sent me to the ER. With my history, they immediately put me on a breathing machine, and started running other tests. I lay helplessly in the bed while a nurse put an IV in my arm.

'What's that for?' my mom asked.

'I was looking over your daughter's history and I'm concerned that she might have a blood clot. She's on birth control for her periods, which puts her at risk of one. With her breathing issues, I'm worried she's going to have a pulmonary embolism. We're going to do an EKG, and if I'm right she's going to need to go into surgery right away.'

I was terrified; a girl at my school had died the year before from a pulmonary embolism. She was dead before the ambulance got there. I started shaking, I was so scared. I couldn't help but bawl my eyes out. I was making the other patients uncomfortable.

A male nurse walked in, with a bunch of wires and stickers. I had seen him around the hospital ever since I could remember. He was cute, and I'd had a crush on him for years. I was so embarrassed when he asked me to remove my shirt to attach the stickers. They hooked me up to the EKG machine, and monitored me for several hours.

The frosty nurse told my mom that there didn't seem to be anything out of the ordinary with my results, but she wanted me to get a CT scan and check my blood. Before they rolled me off, they took blood from my other arm and sent it to the lab for immediate results.

When I got back from the CT scan, the nurse was discussing my lab results with my mom.

'Her white blood cell count is elevated. It looks like she has glandular fever on top of bronchitis,' she said softly.

Mom's mouth curled into a snarl and she exploded, 'You need to apologize to her. We came in to see what was wrong, not to be scared. You start spewing off random bullshit that might be wrong with her, instead of running tests and getting facts.'

Mom always got angry with me, but it was rare that I saw her do it to strangers.

• • •

We went home so I could pack a bag to stay at my grandparents' house again. Even though I felt horrible, I was excited to stay with my grandparents. Mom didn't seem to care either way, like she was too wrapped up in herself to look at the bigger picture. She would be visiting after work every day, bringing by food from the hospital kitchen.

The first thing I did when I arrived was take a hot shower, to loosen my lungs. I wasn't in there long though. Each drop from the shower felt like a rock hitting me, and after just a few minutes, I was exhausted.

I called Adam to let him know I had glandular fever, and that if he wasn't feeling good, he should go to a doctor immediately.

'You keep getting sick because of your house. Can I tell my parents what your house is like to see if they can help?' he said, just as I was about to hang up.

With the little energy I had left, I paused to remember the article I'd read on hoarding. I thought about how I would be blamed for not doing enough to help my mom. I thought about being dragged away from my mom and put into care. But I didn't have enough energy left to fight anymore. I'd been sick so many times, my body was giving in.

'I don't care. If you think they might be able to do something, then go for it,' I said weakly.

• • •

After a week and a half, I was finally well enough to go home. I hated leaving my grandparents' house. I hated going from a clean environment with home-cooked meals, to my house, which was covered in mould and dust, and takeaways and leftovers. Whenever I returned home, I felt like my health was taking two steps back. I'd had bronchitis five times now. It wouldn't take much for me to catch it again. I wished I could live with my grandparents in their clean house, but they always seemed eager for me to go home after I'd been there for several days.

Adam invited me over to his house for a big pot roast dinner that Saturday. It took a lot of convincing, but Mom finally said I could go over. She was worried that I wasn't healthy enough to hang out with Adam.

When I showed up, Will, Lisa and Adam were sitting in the living room, with a whole bunch of pamphlets on their coffee table.

'What's going on? Are we not having dinner anymore?' I asked, looking at their stony faces.

Adam moved over, and patted the seat next to him.

'You said I could tell them about your house,' he said, sweetly. 'I think we might be able to bounce a few ideas off of one another.'

I sat down, but was too embarrassed to look his parents in the eye. I took Adam's hand, and held onto it, tightly.

'So we've heard from Adam how bad it is, but would you mind telling us the state of your house?' his mom Lisa asked.

I started to tell them my Cinderella story, but the words got caught in my throat. Adam squeezed my hand to urge me to talk.

I'd told Adam about my secret because I didn't want to lose him when we were first getting together. The idea of telling grown-ups was scary. It made my situation suddenly very real. I wouldn't be able to hide from it any more.

Adam smiled at me and I tried again. I began with stories of the piles of newspapers, of clothes, of food waste. Instantly, it was like a weight had been lifted off my shoulders. I went on to describe the hole in the roof, my mom's nudity, the laundry room and everything else I could think of.

When I was done talking, Will and Lisa looked sad. Lisa took my free hand and squeezed it. A ghostly silence fell across the room.

'I'm so, so sorry. Why hasn't anyone intervened yet?' she asked.

I stared at the ground. I felt very sad.

'Mom doesn't allow people over, and I haven't told anyone.'

Leaning forward, Will asked, 'Why not though?'

'I'm afraid to. I'm afraid of what people will think of me. And what if they don't think it's that bad? What if they leave me there with her? She'll be so angry I reported her. What would she do to me then?' I explained, close to tears.

Lisa and Will looked at each other.

'Britney, we like you. We don't want to see you suffer anymore. Surely with how sick you've been, the social workers would see that it's a dangerous environment for you to be in. You have a hole in your roof for God's sake. I don't see how they would still let you stay there,' Lisa said.

I felt like a cornered animal, and became defensive.

'Okay, so say I do get taken away, where will I be sent? Child Protective Services is so busy, I'll just be lost in their system. I'll be passed around from foster home to foster home until I'm eighteen. What about my friends? What about Adam? I don't want to give all of that up.'

Adam gave me a hug, and held me tightly.

'What if we were your foster parents?' Will suggested.

Lisa looked at him with a very confused face. After a few seconds, her expression changed and she looked more positive, like the idea had grown on her.

'That just might work,' she said, nodding her head.

I started to feel a kernel of hope.

But then Adam reluctantly piped up.

'That sounds great, but you have to look at the big picture, Mom. We are two months behind on our rent, and neither of you has a job. There's no way the CPS would let us foster Britney.'

Will reluctantly nodded his head in agreement. 'He's right. I'm so sorry Britney. Tell me, what do you want to do?'

'I don't know. It'll almost be easier if I just waited it out until I was eighteen. It's less than three years,' I said, feeling helpless.

Lisa lit a cigarette, and sighed.

'I don't want it to seem like a prison sentence though. This entire situation is awful.'

I looked at them and realised there were no solutions. 'Yeah, I think I'm done with this conversation,' I sighed. The reality was, it was like a prison sentence.

• • •

Lisa drove me home. We sat outside my house for what seemed like ages. Lisa apologised for having to drop me off. Adam kissed me goodbye and I headed back into the hellhole.

When I got upstairs, Mom yelled at me, 'Three minutes until your curfew. You're cutting it close.'

I took off my trainers, and slid my flip-flops on.

'I was in the driveway for a few minutes finishing our conversation,' I answered back, taking a seat on my stool.

'Well, you better not be late,' she said with an attitude.

After a while of watching TV, I felt something stirring inside me. I couldn't concentrate on the screen any longer. I had to get it out. I asked my mom the question I'd be wanting to ask for years, but hadn't had the courage to.

'Mom. Can we clean the house? I mean, really clean it, not just take some trash to Grandma's?'

'Where did that come from?' she looked confused.

'I don't know, I'm just sick of looking at all of this crap,' I said, kicking the trash at my feet.

'Me too, but you've got school and I've got work. What do you suggest?' she asked.

'School and work end at the same time every day, and we have our weekends free. If we get a skip, we should be able to get this place clean,' I said, with some energy.

'Why are you so concerned about all of this now?' she asked, getting angry.

I felt anger rising in my belly. I became defensive, and snapped, 'The house is making me sick. We live like animals. There's a hole in our roof. We just have to throw everything away and start afresh. It'll be the easiest way to—'

'Don't even fucking worry about it. I'll take care of this shit,' she cut me off.

As usual, Mom didn't want to face up to the reality of our situation. I knew she'd do nothing.

It was useless. There was no hope.

CHAPTER 15

A few weeks later, I knocked and waited for someone to answer the door at Adam's house. After a few minutes, I knocked again. Lisa finally answered.

'We called you to come in. You can just come inside, you don't need to knock. You're part of the family.'

Touched, I gave her a hug and said, 'Thanks, you guys make me feel like I belong.'

I sat down at the coffee table and started playing nervously with my hands. It suddenly struck me how anxious I was.

'My mom still hasn't done anything to clean the house, even though she said she would take care of it. If I mention anything about it, she gets angry at me. I can't stand it anymore,' I blurted.

Adam sat down next to me. 'I have something I need to discuss with you.'

'Babe, what's wrong?' I asked, nervously. I could tell from his face it was serious.

'I don't know how to say this,' he took a long look at my face, like he was drinking me in. On the verge of tears, he said, 'We have to move. Our landlord is selling the house and we have to be out of here before she puts it on the market.'

I felt like I had been punched in the stomach.

'Where to? Is it close? When do you have to be out? How will we see each other? I need you Adam,' I trembled.

'It looks like we're moving to the next town. Nothing is set in stone though. We have a month and a half to get things figured out. I'm going to do my best to convince them to stay in the area.' He put his head in his hands and wouldn't look at me.

'I know you'll do your best, but how are we going to see each other? Neither of us has a driving license,' I asked, concerned.

'I'm going to start saving up all of my money from doing odd jobs with Will, and I'm going to pay my mom petrol money so she will come and get you. She likes you and she likes money, she'll do it,' he said confidently.

'He's right, ya know,' Lisa agreed, from the kitchen.

I felt a little better.

'But now I'm not going to be able to sneak over,' I whispered.

Adam laughed, and gave me a kiss.

• • •

The day finally arrived. Adam was moving across town. Instead of being just a few minutes' bike ride, he was now a twenty-minute car ride on the opposite side of town. I rode my bike over to their house, one last time, to help them pack. They had rented a van, and we got to work loading up everything they owned.

I hadn't seen their new house, and was pleasantly surprised when we pulled up to a two storey red brick house in the country. It had four bedrooms, three upstairs and one downstairs, and two bathrooms. The kitchen and living room were huge, and they even had a dining room.

Adam's grandma was going to move in with them, and would take the bottom bedroom, because she couldn't walk up the stairs. It sucked that Adam's bedroom was opposite his parents' room. We weren't going to be able to get any privacy.

It was a long day, but we finally got everything unloaded at the new house. We ordered a few pizzas and pigged out. It was getting close to my curfew, and we had no idea how long it would take to get to my house, so we left a half hour to get me home.

As we drove to mine, I gazed out of the window and thought about how there were not going to be anymore surprise visits after school or late afternoons on the porch, watching the sun set over the trees, or sneaking out in the dead of night. I wouldn't get to see him before or after school anymore, just at the weekend.

But most of all, there was going to be no escape from the trash and my mom. I would have to spend the whole night in that hellhole again. I didn't know how I was going to cope with going back to the way it used to be.

• • •

It had been a while since Adam moved across town, and I was feeling increasingly anxious and upset. I had no escape anymore, other than school. My mom would let me see Adam on Friday nights or on Saturday, but I usually had to figure out how to get there myself. The nearest bus stop was three miles away. Every Saturday morning, I would ride my bike to the grocery store and wait for the bus. The bus took me across town to the closest stop to Adam's. I'd then call Lisa, who would drive four miles to pick me up. The whole process took about two-and-a half-hours – but it was worth it.

Summer was just around the corner, and I couldn't wait. We had Adam's prom, and then Adam would be leaving school and looking for a job. He had worked his butt off to graduate early. My mom would have exploded if I'd left school at sixteen, but Adam's parents were cool.

In the holidays I would be able to see Adam a lot more. I was fifteen so I had started driving lessons. In less than a year I'd have my license and then I would be able to see Adam whenever I wanted.

Just before school let out for the summer, my mom bought me a car. Between tennis, kung fu, babysitting and hanging out with Adam or Nancy, it was becoming too much for her to keep shuttling me around. That was the nicest thing she had ever done for me. Despite her being stretched thin, I wondered if it was a sign that she finally realised how much the trash upset me. If it was her way of helping me out. It was a two-door yellow Honda hatchback. When school broke for the summer she left me the keys, so I could practise driving in our back yard. Of course her generous spirit didn't last.

• • •

A few weeks into the holidays, I was playing at a local tennis club, trying to keep my skills up. I lunged to return serve, but got my footing wrong and ended up doing the splits while leaning forwards.

Somehow I still got the ball over the net, but I couldn't put any weight on my left leg. I stood up, hobbling, and couldn't move when the ball next flew at me. My coach knew something was wrong and he helped me off the court. I had to use him for support.

As I went to sit down on a bench, my hip made a popping noise. When my body weight pressed on my hip, I was in excruciating pain. I stood up, and supported myself on the fence.

'Do you want to rest up, and play again in a bit?' my coach asked concerned.

I fought back the tears and breathed through the pain. 'No, it hurts too much.'

Patting my back he said, 'Maybe you should go to the hospital, you can't even walk. Here, let me get your mom.'

He disappeared around the corner to find my mom, who had been watching me play all this time.

'What's the matter? You only fell down. I didn't pay for you to stand around chatting. Now play!' she ordered.

CHAPTER 15

'Now Gene, she's clearly in pain. She did the surprise splits – something serious might be wrong,' my coach said, crossing his arms as he defended me.

'She just needs to toughen up. She's fine,' Mom walked off, leaving me hobbling.

I spent the rest of the practise time propped up at the side of the court, trying not to put any weight on my left leg. My right leg was getting sore from not moving. I somehow managed to hobble back to the car. The tennis courts were a quarter mile walk away from the parking lot. What normally took me a few minutes, took me half an hour.

When I made it to the car, Mom was annoyed she had been waiting for so long. She became even more annoyed that it took me ten minutes to figure out how I could sit down without being in too much pain. I let out a moan of pain with every bump we hit. The more and more I adjusted myself, the angrier my mom seemed to get. Only when I started crying from the pain of trying to get out of the car did she finally help me.

'If it still hurts tomorrow, I'll take you to the doctors,' she said, supporting me on my right side.

'Can we go to the hospital now? It fucking hurts,' I begged. I was shaking from the pain.

'Watch your mouth, and no, the doctor is much cheaper than the ER,' Mom said, shaking her head.

Step by step, I made it up the stairs. It took forever, and I was exhausted. I wanted to take a shower but we couldn't figure out how to get my leg over the tub. I had lost almost all movement in my leg, and I couldn't support any weight on it. I settled for a cloth wash though my hair was still going to be dusty.

After I got into clean clothes, I had to go to the bathroom. Supporting myself on anything sturdy, I made my way down the hall. I dropped my trousers to my ankles, and attempted to sit on the toilet. I couldn't do it though. Sitting hurt so much, and there was nothing I could hold on to, to lower myself down. To make matters worse, when I went to bend down to pull my trousers up, I couldn't reach my knees, let alone the floor, without almost passing out from the pain.

I burst into tears as I stood there, naked from the waist down. I frantically cried out for my mom.

'I need help going to the bathroom,' I cried.

She quickly rushed down the hallway. I was standing in the bathroom, trying to pull my shirt down over my crotch. She handed me a towel so I could cover myself up. Between sobs, I said, 'I can't sit down to pee and I have to go now.'

'I'm not sure how we're going to be able to do this,' she said, looking around.

Our bathroom was very small. It was a cupboard that had been converted into a bathroom. The toilet was tucked away in the corner, with the sink to its left, no more than two inches from the seat. In front of the toilet and sink, there was the bath. The floor space between them was no more than a foot. In order to sit down on my own, I would have needed to extend my good leg, and carefully lower myself, but there was no room.

I tucked the towel under my armpits and stood in front of the toilet, trying to stifle my cries. I was about to pee myself.

'Ah ha,' Mom said, tapping her head.

She stepped into the bath and said, 'Take my hands, I'm going to lower you onto the toilet.'

I took her hands, struggling to keep the towel up. I hated being naked around my mom, I always felt so vulnerable.

'Britney, I'm not going to look. It'll be a lot easier if you don't worry about the towel,' she told me.

I let the towel drop to the floor. I felt so exposed. I carefully lowered myself onto the toilet. I had to sit with most of my weight on my right butt cheek but I was relieved that I could finally pee. Nothing came out though. I had stage fright with Mom standing there watching me only a foot away.

'Well?' I said, motioning to the door.

'Just holler when you need help up,' she said, leaving the bathroom.

I finally relieved myself when she went into the living room. I went to wipe, only to be thrown back into hysterics, when it was too painful to lean or spread my legs. Hearing me cry, my mom rushed back to help me.

'What now?' she said.

'I can't wipe. What's going to happen if I have to poop? You're not wiping my ass,' I said, crying into my hands.

'I sure as hell won't. Just drip dry for now, we'll figure out what to do about wiping when you actually poop. Do you need help up?' she asked.

Sniffling, I nodded my head. She got in the bath again, grabbed my hands and hoisted me off the toilet. She started walking away when I quietly said, 'I can't pick my pants up.'

She turned around to face me, but couldn't help but laugh.

'I'm sorry kiddo. I'm not laughing at you, but it's

kind of funny just how pathetic all of this is,' she said through snorts.

I started crying again. I felt so vulnerable and disgusting.

'I'm not pathetic, if I could do it myself I would,' I sobbed.

'That's not what I meant. The situation is pathetic, not you. Here, I'll help you to bed,' she said, putting her arm around my shoulder.

I hopped to my room, and carefully lay down. No matter what I did, I couldn't get comfortable. The best position was to lie on my good side, with my leg elevated. My mom made a mound of pillows and blankets, and gently rested my leg on it. She then tucked blankets around my back so I wouldn't roll over. I took four ibuprofens and tried to fall asleep.

I lay awake for the entire night, constantly making small adjustments to get comfortable. Any time I slightly moved my hips, pain shot down my leg and up my stomach. Every time Mom got up to go to the bathroom, she'd peek her head in to check on me, and every time I reminded her how much pain I was in. Finally she agreed to help me.

'When the doctor's office opens up, I'll call and make an appointment,' she said reluctantly.

I couldn't wait to go to the doctors. I was really hoping they would give me something for the pain and that they'd figure out what was wrong. The clock finally ticked over to 9 a.m., and I hollered at my mom.

'The doctor's office is open, call them now,' I pleaded.

I could hear her slowly go to the bathroom, then to the living room, and shuffle around some papers as she tried to find the doctors number amongst the trash. She finally rang them, and I heard her yelp, 'Immediately, is it really that serious?' After a few seconds, she hung up, and came into my room.

'The doctor wants to see you now,' she said, pulling my blankets back. She helped me sit up and slide out of bed.

'I have to go to the bathroom,' I said, doing a one-legged potty dance.

Once again we did the routine where she got in the bathtub and lowered me onto the toilet. I had needed to pee for hours, and couldn't wait until she got out of the bathroom to relieve myself. Then my cellphone rang. It was Adam, asking if I wanted to hang out.

'I can't. I hurt my hip playing tennis yesterday.

I have to go to the doctors,' I said, feeling very upset.

'Are you going to be okay?' he asked, concerned.

'I'm not sure. We are going to the doctors right now,' I said, quietly.

'Okay, well I'm going to let you go then. Call me when you know what's up. I love you,' he said sweetly.

'I will, I love you too,' I said, hanging up.

• • •

When we showed up at the doctor's surgery, he took a quick look and told Mom off.

'Gene, you really should have taken her to the ER yesterday when it happened. It astonishes me that you didn't. She needs to go to the ER right now to have X-rays taken.'

It was like his words had fallen on deaf ears. Mom shrugged them off and pretended she had taken the right course of action. It was the same way she handled the bedbugs, the bronchitis and the glandular fever. She never wanted to accept responsibility for my pain and suffering.

The X-rays showed that I had fractured my hip, and that there was nothing I could do but to stay as still as possible for three weeks. Upon being discharged, I was told to take ibuprofen for the pain,

I didn't need any stronger medicine. I was advised not to walk unless I had to go to the bathroom. I had to stay in bed and rest. On our way home, we rented crutches from a pharmacy so I could get to the bathroom and kitchen while Mom was at work.

A feeling of dread rose in me. *I'm going to be stuck in the house twenty-four hours a day, no escape. Just the trash and me.* I felt sick.

• • •

Once we got home, I tried getting comfortable on my bed, but it was useless. All of the blankets I used to prop my legs up would shift or go flat after a while. I was going to go insane from boredom, not being able to do anything but lie in bed for three weeks. As my mom was adjusting my pillows, she suggested an alternative.

'You know, you can stay in my room until your hip heals. You really liked the position you lay in while you in the hospital. The dip in my bed would probably be really close to that.'

I cringed at the thought of staying in her room for three weeks. The hole was still in the roof, the rubbish was level with the bed and I really didn't want to lie in her piss hole. We got rid of her last mattress because the middle had caved in, but her new one already had a crater in it.

'No, thanks. I'll figure something out,' I said, shaking my head defiantly.

'Okay, but the offer is still out there. And I have a TV, you won't be as bored in my room,' she said, walking out into the hall.

The next day before she left for work, she popped her head in, to check on me.

'Are you going to be all set in here?' she asked.

I was exhausted because I couldn't fall asleep.

'I'm fine. I'll see you after work. Bring back something sweet?'

Laughing, she said, 'Will do. See ya later.'

Every time I fell asleep, I kept trying to roll over, causing me to move or put pressure on my hip. I tried sleeping the entire morning, but the sun was shining directly in my eyes, and there was no way I could get up to close my curtains. At 11 a.m. I had to go to the bathroom. I hadn't gone to the bathroom on my own yet, I was scared I would wet myself without my mom's help.

I rolled over onto my belly and pulled myself carefully off the bed and onto the ground. Using a crutch and my bed, I picked myself up and started heading for the bathroom. I was only using one crutch to support my weight on my left side. When

I leaned on the crutch, it slipped out from underneath me and I fell on my hip.

'Fucking, fuck,' I cried out, punching the floor.

I looked around and saw that my crutch had landed on the corner of a trash bag that was in the hallway. It must have slipped when I put my weight on it. I grabbed the crutch and used it to pull myself up. I carefully made my way to the bathroom and started screaming when I couldn't lower myself onto the toilet. I looked at the bath and took my clothes off. I used the crutch to support myself as I climbed into it.

I placed the crutch just outside the shower, and turned the taps on. I peed quickly, letting the shower rinse me off from the waist down. I grabbed the crutch and hobbled onto the bathroom floor. Using the hooked end of a hanger, I had no choice but to pick a dirty towel from off the ground, and dried myself off as best as I could. I cringed with every stroke across my skin. I couldn't reach just below my knees, though, so the lower half of my legs stayed wet. Lining my feet up with the leg holes in my trousers, I used the same hanger to pull them up.

I began hobbling back to my room, when I paused outside my mom's room. I inspected the sheets from the hallway, they didn't look wet. My mom didn't always piss her bed, sometimes she went through a dry spell. *Maybe I'd get lucky this time?* I felt her blankets for wetness – nothing, they were all dry. I propped myself on the crutch while I spread out her blankets in such a way that they covered the hole.

One by one, I grabbed the blankets and pillows from my room, and tossed them onto my mom's bed. I put my least favourite blanket over my mom's blanket and then then sunk my exhausted body into the crater in her bed. My hip felt a million times better being elevated. I propped my back up with a pillow, and it felt like I was in the hospital bed. A smelly hospital bed.

I grabbed the remote, flicked on the TV and flipped through the channels. Daytime TV sucked, so I settled for midday game shows. After a few minutes my eyelids grew heavy and rolled down like shutters. I was finally comfortable enough that I could sleep.

• • •

The next thing I knew, Mom was shaking me awake.

'So I see you took me up on my offer. Here's cookies, brownies and ice cream,' she said, tossing a big paper bag at me.

I tore open the bag and grabbed a brownie, dipping it in the tub of ice cream.

'Mmm, these are good,' I said, through chews.

'Those are my walnut toffee brownies. You must be hungry, I know we don't have anything to eat here,' she said, handing me another bag.

I looked through the new bag and found a tray full of baked chicken breasts, two takeaway containers of mashed potatoes, gravy, three slices of lasagne and a Styrofoam bowl of taco soup. I opened the taco soup and sipped it straight from the bowl.

'Ah, my favourite,' I said wiping the corners of my lips. 'Thanks Mom,' I smiled. When she was being nice, everything seemed better.

Mom went to the living room and left me to flip through the channels. I snoozed off again, but woke up to the sound of water pouring into the buckets. It must have started raining while I was asleep. When the wind blew just right, I got sprayed with some water. Disgusted, I fell back into the hole, blocking myself from the rain with an extra blanket.

I looked around and I just wanted to scream. No amount of cakes and sweets could take me away from the grim reality. Mom's room was filthy, it smelled really bad, I was getting soaked and I couldn't see Adam. I didn't want to spend my summer in my mom's bed. I wanted to hang out with Adam and forget about everything else in my life.

I lay there worrying about stupid stuff – like whether Adam would go off me while I was trapped in the house. He couldn't visit me. Mom locked up the house when she left every day, and I couldn't get to the door to unlock it. I also worried if I would get ill again. With every growing fear, all I could hear was the rain getting louder and louder, like someone drumming on my ears.

• • •

It had been three long, boring weeks, but I was finally able to walk on my own, and I could put pressure back on my hip. As I walked outside for the first time, I took a big deep breath, savouring the fresh air. I carried a blanket and threw it across the old mattress which was still on the porch. After being trapped in Mom's room upstairs, her old mattress outside didn't seem so bad – and at least it had been aired for the last few months. I lay back and watched the clouds pass by as I talked to Adam on the phone.

We made plans to hang out that weekend. My mom was going to drop me off early in the morning and not pick me up until midnight. I was so excited that I finally got to see Adam. I had missed him so much.

The day before, I braved it and took a bike ride over to my church. It was about a mile away, tucked back in the woods. I liked riding my bike through the trees, and I was desperate to talk to someone other than my mom. When I showed up, my youth group leader was there and had a big bonfire, roaring. He was glad to see me because I hadn't been to church in a month. To celebrate my hip healing, we got stuff to make marshmallows and hot dogs.

At 6 p.m. he drove me back home with my bike, so I didn't have to make the journey again when it was dark. I was tired after a long day outside and I went straight to bed. Then, in the middle of the night, I woke up coughing. I couldn't breathe. My lungs were on fire, and I was bringing up green phlegm with blood streaked through it.

I broke down in tears because I didn't need a doctor to tell me what was wrong. The damp and the cold had attacked my weak lungs.

Mom took me to the hospital where I was put on a breathing treatment. I had bronchitis again. I turned my head to face the wall. I couldn't look at her while I lay helplessly in the hospital bed. *I hated her.*

My fear of getting sick had become a reality. Adam and I were going to have to postpone.

CHAPTER 15

Some summer holiday. Grandma and grandpa were on vacation, and Mom didn't want to burden my aunt for a week. I was trapped in the house again.

There was no escape.

CHAPTER 16

Adam and I found a way to feel like we were together even when we were miles apart.

For my sixteenth birthday, my mom had got me a portable DVD player. Every movie Adam got, he got a second copy, so we could 'watch' a movie together. We started the movies at the same time, and stayed on the phone, silently watching and commenting occasionally as to what was going on.

I was allowed to have the DVD player in my room during summer break, but once school started it needed to be in the living room. Knowing 'movie night' would only last a few weeks, we made the best of it. It was our way of being together and it transported me away from the trash by my feet.

A few days later, Lisa rang my house phone. When I answered she said, 'Hey hon. Can I talk to your mom?'

Skeptically, I handed the phone over. 'It's Lisa. She wants to talk to you.'

Taking the phone, my mom rolled her eyes at me. 'What did you do now?' she said.

She went to her room so she could talk with Lisa in private.

I was really nervous. I had no idea why Lisa wanted to talk to my mom. Given everything she knew about the hoarding, Lisa didn't care for her too much. I turned the TV down, trying to see if I could make out anything Mom was saying. My hands started to get clammy, and my stomach was churning.

My mom finally came back into the living room, sarcastically laughing and shaking her head.

'That woman is fucking crazy,' she said, hanging up the phone.

'Why? What did you two talk about?' I asked, hesitantly.

'She wanted to know if you could spend the night, and watch the meteor shower over the weekend. Does my forehead have "stupid" written across it?' Mom said, still laughing.

'Why can't I?' I asked, confused.

'You really have to ask? Because you're dating her son – who will also be sleeping there. Fuck no. That's a recipe for disaster.'

'It's not like we're going to have sex. His parents are going to be there,' I lied.

'I said no. Drop it,' she said, sternly.

• • •

I was still allowed to go over to Adam's house on Saturday, but I had to be home by 11 p.m. We were playing video games when I noticed that I had a half hour to get home. Not wanting to be late, I packed up the controller and turned off the Xbox. Adam grabbed my hips and pulled me in closer.

'But I don't want you to go,' he kissed my shoulder, and hugged me tightly.

I wiggled loose and pushed him away. I was too afraid of my mom's wrath.

'I know, but if I'm not home on time, I won't be able to see you for a while,' I explained.

• • •

We had travelled a few miles down the road when an ambulance and a fire truck roared up behind us. We stopped to let them pass, and noticed several police cars coming down the road. We didn't move, and waited for them to pass us before we continued.

A few more miles down the road, we came across a road block. Lisa was stopped by the police officer.

'Sorry ma'am, you're going to have to turn around.

There's a house fire, and the road is completely blocked,' the cop signalled.

I only had fifteen minutes to get home, and we were still twenty minutes away. Nervous, I asked Lisa to step on it. We rolled through stop signs, ran red lights and drove over the speed limit. I kept trying to call Mom, but she was using the internet, so the house phone didn't work. She wasn't answering her mobile. I left her a bunch of messages, letting her know I was going to be late because of the road block. My heart was racing.

Amazingly, Lisa did it though. We pulled into the driveway at 10.57 p.m. I gave Adam a kiss and they took off. Before I went inside, I saw Mom's car window was open, so I rolled it up and approached the house. As I was walking up to the porch, I saw that laundry was hung over the rails. Our dryer had broken the week before, and Mom was waiting until her next paycheck to get it fixed.

I gathered up an armful of clothes, and groped for the front doorknob, because I couldn't see past the heap of laundry in my arms. I finally opened the door and yelled out.

'Hey Mom, I'm home.'

'You're one minute late,' she said in a glacial voice. She made me jump. I dropped the clothes because

I wasn't expecting her to be standing in the door frame at the top of the stairs. I tried to pick them up and explain.

'Oh, no, we actually pulled up at 10.57. I was just rolling up—'

'I said be home by 11 o'fucking clock. It's now 11.01. You're a minute late,' she boomed.

I was astounded at how ridiculous she was being. I carried on picking up the clothes – *her* clothes.

'I'm clearly not late. If you would have let me finish my sentence earlier, you would have known—'

She tried interrupting me, 'I'm your mother, don't talk to me that way.'

I just talked over her, though, speaking more loudly, desperate to be heard.

'I rolled up *your* car window because you would have just sent me back out to do it later, and I grabbed all of the clothes off the porch. If I was a minute late I wouldn't have had any time to do all that. So, tell me again about how I was late?'

She stood at the top of the stairs, racking her brain for words. She looked down at me, but I could only see her silhouette. The stairwell was dark and the light from the living room was shining around her. She finally got me where she knew it would hurt.

'I need to know you're home on time. It's your

fault that you decided to do those things, but in my book, you're late. You didn't walk into this house until 11.01, which is one minute late. Until I can trust you with a curfew again, you're grounded from seeing Adam, for a month.'

I felt crushed.

'Fuck this, and fuck you,' I said, dropping the clothes and walking outside. I rolled down my mom's window, knowing there was going to be rain in the night. When I came back in the house, she wasn't in the doorway anymore. I picked up my clothes, and stepped all over hers with my dirty shoes.

I hated her.

When I got upstairs, she was sitting on the couch. Without looking at me she carried on with her attack.

'You know. I cart your ass around. I let you see him whenever you want, and you still treat me like this. I simply asked you to be home by a certain time and you're late.'

'You're fucking late to everything,' I screamed at her. 'Do you know how many laps I've run in sports for being late? How is it my fault when I don't even fucking drive? Grab your fucking phone – you'll see that I tried calling you to let you know there was a possibility of being late. There was a house fire and the road was blocked. How am I supposed to fucking control that?'

Those words felt amazing to say. Years of pent-up anger finally exploded out of my chest. I stormed off to my room. I was so angry, but I couldn't slam my door – because I didn't have one. I couldn't hit anything; I couldn't scream into a pillow, I couldn't even call Adam, because my mom would be listening. I felt so trapped.

From the living room, Mom yelled, 'You can go fuck yourself.'

I yelled back, 'And so can you!'

We never talked about what happened that night again. We pretended like it never happened. Just like we pretended we didn't live in squalor.

• • •

After school one day I went to the hospital, instead of home. I had a lot of homework, and I liked being able to use the tables in the cafeteria instead of trying to balance my work on the arm of the couch. When I went into the kitchen, my mom handed me an envelope.

'Emily wanted me to give this to you,' she said, handing me an envelope. Emily was a neighbour who wanted me to babysit her two kids. I had to delay working for Emily because it would mean taking the kids to after-school sports, and I couldn't afford to take my driving test yet.

'What is it?' I asked, tearing it open.

Mom shook her head and shrugged her shoulders. 'I don't have the slightest clue.'

I pulled the card out of the envelope. The front of it read: 'Thanks for being you!' When I opened the card, a bunch of $20 notes fell to the ground. I scrambled to pick them up.

'What the fuck is that for? You haven't babysat for a while,' Mom snarled.

Inside the card, Emily had written, 'I really need you driving the boys. Here's the rest of the money so you can take the test.' I couldn't believe what I was reading as I said it out loud.

'She just gave you over a hundred dollars so you can start working for her sooner?' Mom asked, upset.

'Yeah, how awesome is that? I'm going to schedule my test for the end of the week,' I squealed. Someone was looking out for me after all.

Mom stopped me in my tracks. She was clearly jealous.

'Excuse me. No you're not. I still haven't forgotten about how you ran a red light with me a couple of months ago, and you were late for a curfew. Just because she gave you the money, doesn't mean you can take the test,' Mom spat.

Why is she trying to block every escape route I can find? I hate her so much.

'She gave me the money so I can take the test as soon as possible, not sit on it until you decide I'm ready. I'm taking the test,' I said, determined. I'd spent a whole summer trapped in her bedroom being ill, there was no way she was going to stop me escaping.

'Oh really, who is going to ride with you? You need a parent in the car in order to take the test.'

'Oh really? Then why does my guide book say I can have any licensed family member over twenty-one ride with me. I called Grandpa and he said he would take me to the test,' I fought back.

'You're lying,' she said, agitated.

'You wish I was,' I said, walking out the door. I had found my voice and I could taste the freedom already.

•••

I booked my test for after school. My mom would be at work and wouldn't be able to stop me. Grandpa picked me up in my car, and we went to the test centre. I passed the written test, and was just about to start the driver's test, when Mom called.

'Good luck kiddo,' she said, sweetly. 'I'll take you to the driver's license office after I get out of work. You should be able to drive to school tomorrow.'

I didn't know what had turned her around, but I was glad of it. As long as she didn't get in the way of my license – my freedom – I was happy.

I lost one point in the preliminary test because I hit the cone while parallel parking, but I still passed. The rest of the test was a breeze, I passed with flying colours. I called my mom.

'We're going to the driver's license office. I passed my test!' I said, excitedly.

'Awesome, we'll go as soon as my shift is over,' she said.

My grandma joined Grandpa and I at a local hot dog restaurant, to celebrate my passing. I didn't eat very much, I was so excited. I had butterflies in my stomach because I was about to get my license – my ticket out of the squalor. I daydreamed about hitting the open road with the music blaring, driving far away from all my problems. Grandma had to say my name several times to get me back into the room, I was so far away. We finished our food and Grandpa dropped me off at the hospital and parked my car while I ran in to find Mom.

As I was waiting for her shift to finish, I tried focusing on homework, but I was too distracted. After what seemed like forever, Mom grabbed me and we left for the license office. As they took my picture, I had the biggest grin on my face. I was finally free.

In the car park, I begged my mom to allow me to go and see Adam.

'Not now, it's too late. And, you've only just got your license, you need it to settle first,' she said, shaking her head.

Her words were like a pin to my balloon of happiness. I deflated back into my seat.

'But you're going to let me drive to school tomorrow morning. Why not now?' I asked, frustrated at her reasoning.

'You can go tomorrow after school, but not now,' she said sitting in the driver's seat.

She dropped me off at the hospital so I could grab my car. As I was sitting in the driver's seat she leaned in the window.

'Follow me. I want to be able to see you,' she ordered.

I rolled my eyes and nodded my head obediently. I started my car and heard it purr. My heart fluttered; this was my car that I could finally legally drive. I flicked through the radio station until I found a song

I liked and put the car in drive. I followed Mom home the entire way, doing everything perfectly. I couldn't help but smile as it wouldn't be long now.

I ran upstairs and called Adam.

'Guess who finally has her license?' I asked, excited.

'Fuck yeah. Good job babe. You should come over, now,' he said, happy.

'I can't. I've already asked. But after school tomorrow I'll be at your house.'

• • •

I woke up, and turned off my alarm. I had over an hour before school started and it was only a fifteen minute drive. I watched the news until it was time to leave, impatiently tapping my feet against the floor the whole time. I woke Mom up just to say goodbye, hoping she would be too tired to lecture me about driving safely.

Just before I pulled out of the driveway, I called Nancy.

'I got my license last night. I'm going to pick you up,' I said, holding back my excitement.

'Oh my God, you're my life saver. I actually just woke up a few minutes ago and would have missed the bus. I'll buy coffee if you want to stop,' she said, enthusiastically.

'Awesome, I'll be there in a few,' I said, hanging up. I swung by Nancy's house, and we went past the drive-through of a local coffee shop. Sipping on my chai tea latte, we made it to school on time.

● ● ●

After school, I raced to Adam's house. He lived half an hour away from my high school, but I made it there in twenty minutes.

I opened the door and was greeted by the dogs.

'Hey it's Britney!' I called out, petting their heads.

Adam came down the stairs, surprised to see me.

'I'm so bored. I wish we could do something,' he groaned.

'We can silly. I have a car. Let's go!' I said, without a care in the world.

'That's right,' he said, excited.

He ran up to his parents' room and told them he was stepping out with me for a while. Will came outside to give my car a look over. After deeming it safe, Adam and I took off.

'Where do you want to go?' I asked, smiling.

I felt in charge of my own destiny.

'I know just where to go,' Adam perked up. 'I built a really awesome fort in the woods when I was a kid. It might still be there.'

I wound down my window and let the fresh air rush over me as Adam gave turn by turn directions. As we travelled into the countryside, open fields replaced the built up roads. With every mile we drove, I felt a hundred miles away from my problems.

We turned into the car park of a wood. I grabbed a blanket and we started hiking. Carefully studying the trees, Adam followed the trail he had left almost a decade ago. When Adam and some friends had built the fort, deep into the woods, they had carved arrows on trees to lead them to it. It took time, but we found the first arrow and continued onwards. After hiking for half an hour, Adam started jumping up and down and pointing.

'There it is. There it is,' he said running towards it.

Between two trees, there was a crude fort built out of sticks and branches. On the outside it was fifteen feet long and at least ten feet wide. We crawled in through the opening near the trunk of one of the trees. I could stand up and not worry about hitting my head. Adam on the other hand, had to duck a bit.

As I was laying down the blanket, Adam crawled outside, to make sure it was just the two of us. He came back in and hit his head on the low ceiling.

'Cover your eyes,' he said.

I pulled my hood over my face, and tucked myself into the corner of the fort. I could hear Adam pushing, and branches falling. After a few minutes, Adam said, 'Ta da!'

He had taken the entire ceiling down so we were only surrounded by walls. One side he had made lower so I could peek over the wall if I stood on my tiptoes. Adam picked up the blanket and shook it off, then lay down and grabbed my hips and pulled me to the ground. It felt so primitive making love outside. I was so in tune with the world around me, looking past Adam, and seeing the clouds float by.

As I gazed at the sky above – I felt free.

CHAPTER 17

For my seventeenth birthday I got a Wii from my grandparents. It was the first video game console I'd ever owned and I was really excited. When we got home that Saturday, I ran to set it up. Suddenly, I realised, I wasn't going to have room to play it for all the trash. I started cleaning up the living room.

As Mom wouldn't let me throw much away, I neatly stacked rubbish in piles and she went to watch the TV in her bedroom. By the time I had made enough room to play, I was exhausted. I sat on the couch and ate dinner. It made me smile to see a good portion of the living room floor. I couldn't remember the last time I'd seen it. I then played with the Wii in my new clean area for a few hours before going to bed.

In the morning I was woken up by the sun and excited to play more video games. But when I went to the living room, I was greeted with a messy floor again. Nothing as bad as it was, but it looked like Mom had riffled through the piles of trash, letting things spew out where they fell.

I stormed to her room and woke her up.

'What happened in the living room? I worked for hours getting it clear,' I shouted. I was mad.

'I was looking for something,' she mumbled, still half asleep.

'This is bullshit,' I said walking away, pissed off.

I went back to the living room. I was kicking the garbage back to the sides of the room when I thought: *Who the fuck cares. Mom's sleeping so she'll let me go to Adam's*. I'd stopped caring.

I got dressed, put my shoes on and grabbed my purse. I stopped outside my mom's room and waited until she snored really loudly. She finally let out a roar.

'I'm going to Adam's. Is it okay if I'm back by eleven?' I asked.

Startled, she barely opened her eyes, and smacked her lips. Dozing back to sleep she said, 'Yeah, that's fine. You know what? Make it eleven thirty. Oh, and hang out the blankets in the wash downstairs.'

Before she could say anything else, I was down the stairs, and quickly moving the loads of laundry. When dryer had broken the previous year, instead of fixing or replacing it, Mom decided we could just hang our clothes all over the house to dry – wherever we could find a place. We slung them over the back of the couch and computer chair. We hung underwear from the ceiling fan, or over lamp shades. I hated drying our clothes like this, because it took them forever to dry, dirt always got on them and they smelled terrible.

I hung out the last blanket, and bolted for my car. I called Adam.

'Hey, I'm on my way over. And I don't have to be home until eleven thirty.'

'How did you do that?' he exclaimed, shocked.

'I waited until she was out cold, and then asked if I could come over,' I proudly told him. 'She always says yes if she's sleeping when I ask her.'

Laughing, Adam said, 'Awesome, I'll see you soon.'

As I pulled out of the driveway, my car chugged, and I rolled to a stop in the middle of the road. A car was approaching, so I frantically turned the key, over and over. After a few seconds of trying, my car finally roared to life, and I quickly backed it into the driveway, where it died again.

What the hell? I just put gas in it last night and Grandpa changed the oil a month ago, I thought, turning the key again. This time, the engine wouldn't even start.

I got in my mom's car instead, and headed to Adam's house. When I pulled up, Adam was sitting on the porch. I could see him start to panic. I waved to him as I pulled into the driveway. He seemed relieved, and sat down again.

'You scared the hell out of me,' Adam spluttered as I walked towards him. 'I was smoking a joint when I saw you. I thought you would be your mom.'

I laughed and took a perch next to him. I lit a cigarette and took in the moment.

'Nope. Just me. My car broke.'

Exhaling his puff, he said, 'That sucks. I wanted to go for a drive today, if you know what I mean.'

'Yeah, no back seat to "play" in. It's the worst I've ever seen it,' I said, shaking my head.

We only had twelve hours to hang out together before I had to get the car back. Lisa and Will had just got a new puppy, so we played with him for part of the day, then I took him into town to fill out applications for jobs.

As he was writing references in, Adam turned to me, with a serious expression on his face.

'I'm going to find a job that pays well, so when you graduate we can get a place of our own. I want you to be able to leave that house when you are eighteen.'

I leaned over and gave him kiss on the cheek.

'I love you,' I said, smiling.

I couldn't wait for the day I could leave.

• • •

A few weeks went by, and Adam hadn't heard from any of the jobs he'd applied for. It was a small town, and the pickings were slim.

I was still driving my mom's car, because my grandpa said my car had blown a head gasket. I missed that car so much, it was my ticket to freedom and it was clean. My grandparents had a spare car, which they lent to my mom. Mom had lent me her old banger. I know she was trying to be nice, but it was so full of shit that none of my friends could fit in the back. It also smelled like death; something inside was rotting. I tried to empty the car but Mom kept screaming at me when she noticed things were missing. It was hopeless.

I needed that car to be clean when I took the boys I was babysitting to summer camp. I had to do it so my mom didn't know, so I pulled up to a car wash, picked the cubicle that was in the back corner and started emptying the contents of the car. I had already filled two trash bags when one of the attendants came over.

'We need you to leave. You've filled several trash bins but have only spent $1 on a vacuum.'

I was embarrassed. I could feel my cheeks blush.

'I'm sorry, it's not even my car, it's my mom's. I just ...' I trailed off and hopped back in the front seat and took off.

As I was driving home, I realised it was trash night at Adam's house. I made a U-turn – I'd just passed the road that took me to Adam's.

Lisa was outside, smoking, when I pulled up.

'It's a surprise to see you,' she said, smiling.

'Yeah, I'm supposed to be cleaning the car right now. I've got to babysit tomorrow but I have no room in the back to put the kids and their stuff,' I explained, opening the back door.

I rolled their rubbish bin over, and started throwing more stuff away. I finally had the seat clear, and was working on the floor space in the back, when I pulled back a crumpled grocery bag to reveal the major source of smell. I gingerly opened the takeaway box to reveal a thick, gloopy, brown sludge. Gagging, I quickly threw it in the trash, and gasped for air. *How could my mom not notice that smell?*

Hearing me cough, Adam came outside. He gave me a kiss.

'How long have you been here?'

'Ten minutes maybe. I've got to get my car cleaned,' I shrugged.

Adam flashed me a sympathetic smile and peered into the back seat.

'Argh,' he exclaimed, covering his nose with his hand. The smell of rotten sludge still lingered.

He leaned in again and grabbed an armful of rubbish for the bin. After twenty minutes, with the two of us clearing out the back, it was finally empty. There were still wrappers stuck to the carpet, dirt rubbed into the fabric, and the floor of the entire back seat area was wet, but at least the boys could sit down in it.

I grabbed my keys and unlocked the trunk.

'We still have room in the bin, may as well empty this too,' I said.

I rolled the bin to the back of the car. As soon as the boot opened, you could smell the mould and mildew. I held my breath and stepped back. When I thought I was far away enough to get fresh air, I started breathing again. Lisa had come over to get a closer look at what could be smelling so bad.

The trunk was much harder to clean, because not everything was trash, even if it looked like it. My mom sometimes did charity work, teaching art and crafts to small kids at the church, and the boot was full with all of her snacks, lesson plans and crafts. I pulled everything church related out and placed it in a pile next to Lisa. She kicked the juice boxes and bucket of animal crackers in disbelief.

'Did your mom really hand out snacks to the kids that were sitting in that nasty, dirty trunk?' she gasped.

Pulling out a mouldy towel I hadn't seen in years, I said, 'Yep.'

We dug out books which were sodden, clothes, shoes, empty drinks bottles, full soda bottles. It was hard to determine what some things were, they were so disintegrated. I wiped the sweat from my forehead and turned to Adam.

'Can you take out the spare tyre? There's more shit underneath it.'

I leaned on the side of the trunk to catch my breath and watched as Adam pulled it out. He hadn't even pulled it out of the trunk when we were all swarmed with albino fruit flies. Adam dropped the tyre and ran away, trying to swat them from his face. I covered my mouth and took a step back, bewildered at the hundreds of flies. They were albino, every single one of them. So many generations of fruit flies had lived in the darkness of the trunk that they had stopped producing pigment. I was disgusted.

• • •

The next day, I picked up the boys who I babysat and drove them to their camps. The younger one was about to sit in the back seat when he froze, and dug his heels in.

'Buddy, what's wrong?' I asked.

Folding his arms he said, 'It's sticky. Where's *your* car?'

'I know it's gross. My car has broken down, this is what I've got now,' I said, laying a towel across the seat.

'Is that better?' I asked, smoothing out the towel.

Nodding his head, he hopped in and buckled up. Their camp was at my high school, which was perfect, because I had a TV club meeting there at the same time. I parked the car in my usual spot, made sure the boys got to where they needed to go and I rushed to the studio, taking a seat in the back.

I didn't care what the teacher was saying, I had just joined the club to get away from my mom and the house.

The next day when I checked the mail, there was a blank envelope on top of the regular mail. Curious,

I ripped it open. Inside was a gift certificate for a car cleaning company and a note:

> Brit
> I know the mess in the car isn't your fault, and I appreciate you taking the time to clear out the junk. The boys told me how much it smelled though. You've been a godsend running them everywhere, and I figured you would want the car cleaned (as do my boys haha).
> Emily

I was so excited that I booked an appointment the very next day. I dropped it off at the garage, and when the guys opened the doors and trunk they were at a loss for words.

As I walked away, I cringed when I heard one whisper, 'Dude, this is the nastiest fucking car I've ever seen.'

I was in shock when I picked it back up. The car looked like new, and you could only smell a fresh lemon scent. *I'm going to keep this car as clean as possible from now on.*

• • •

Mom wouldn't let me drive to Adam's very much anymore. She'd started to not like Adam, I think because he was taking me away from her. I could never understand how one minute she wanted to be my best friend, and the next, she was mean to me.

I'd signed up for any club that would take me at the start of the new school year. If I couldn't go to Adam's house, then all my free time would be spent at school. I would even volunteer to drive other club members home after events, just to kill more time. People thought I was being nice, but what I was really doing was escaping. Every person I drove home was a few more minutes I didn't have to spend in *that* house.

Eventually, my desperate efforts to get away became too much for me to cope with. I was exhausted all the time, and on the verge of getting ill. So I called on the help of my friends to make up excuses for me. I asked Nancy if she would cover for me. I told Mom I was going to her house, when I was really sneaking off to Adam's. She gave me no choice but to lie.

My mom always wanted me to call her when I got to Nancy's house, so I had to come up with a way to fool her. I'd ring Nancy from Adam's house, and ask her be quiet while I opened a third line to my mom. Every once in a while, Nancy would hold the phone away, and say something, so it seemed like she was with me. If my mom wanted to talk with Nancy, we would pretend to pass the phone, and then Nancy would start talking with my mom. Nancy would 'hand' the phone back to me until my mom and I were finished talking. It worked every time, and I never got caught. But I hated how duplicitous she had made me become.

The Christmas holidays were coming up, and we only had half a day of school for the remainder of the week. I'd finished my homework for the year, and didn't have any tests until the end of the week. I asked Mom if I could go to Adam's house.

'No, you got a B in Biology, you need to do your homework,' she said, annoyed with me again.

'My homework *is* done. And besides, that's the only class I have a B in,' I protested.

'B *minus*,' she interrupted.

I desperately tried to fight my corner.

'I have As in the rest of my classes. And the biology class I'm taking is a college class standard. So, not only am I getting a good grade in a hard class, but I'm also getting college credits.'

Pursing her lips, she said, 'No. Go to the library and study.'

'Fine,' I said, leaving the hospital.

I defiantly went to Adam's house, anyway. My mom's work schedule hadn't changed in eight years.

If I got home before she left work, she would never know.

• • •

I called Adam, to let him know I was heading over, but nobody answered. I pulled up outside his house, and I was relieved to see the family car in the driveway. I'd come over unannounced many times when nobody had been in. This was one of those times when I really needed Adam. I walked in, and the dogs started barking excitedly.

'It's just me,' I called out, slipping my shoes off and petting the dogs.

Adam appeared around the corner. He looked serious.

'We need to talk,' he said.

'Uh oh, what's wrong?' I asked playfully, even though I was nervous on the inside. I hated change and I could feel something was in the air.

We went to his bedroom and I took the bull by the horns.

'What's up?' I blurted.

'I found a job!' His face lit up. 'But I won't start for a few months.'

I sat up, excited for him.

'That's amazing. Where? And why don't you start for a few months?'

He took my hands and looked directly into my eyes. 'Well, that's what we need to talk about. It's not for a few months because it's a seasonal job.'

'That's fine, it'll give you a chance to make some money while looking for another job,' I said, still bubbly.

'Right, but – it's in Utah. Jerry and I are going to work at a four star restaurant. They have cabins for us to live in,' he finally confessed.

I was lost for words. Adam was my everything. He was the love of my life, and my sanctuary away from that prison of a home. He was going to be hundreds of miles away, states away, living it up with his best friend.

'When are you going? You're not going to miss prom or my graduation, are you? What about when I turn eighteen? I thought we were going to start a life together?' The tears welled in my eyes.

I swallowed hard as he delivered the bad news.

'I'm leaving in April. I have to be there the first week of May. I won't be back until November.'

I frantically shook my head. I couldn't believe this was happening to me. Suddenly my hurt turned to anger.

'You're going to miss the most important moments of my life. I was there for yours,' I said, hurt.

'You want me to miss out on this opportunity? I have never left the state, you've been to China. What's the difference?' he snapped, coldly.

'That was just a holiday though. I don't understand how you think this is okay?' I said, on the verge of tears.

'I don't understand how you think it's okay to hold me back? I want to go on an adventure, I want to do things. What's going to happen when you graduate? You're going to go to college and still be under your mom's control,' he said angrily.

His words were like a javelin through my heart. *Under my mom's control? How could he?*

'Don't go,' I begged. 'You can have an adventure with me. It's not my fault that I'm not eighteen yet. Just wait until my birthday, then it'll be just you and me.'

Adam pulled me close, for a hug.

'I'm not leaving for a while, and it's not set in stone anyway. We need to find the money to get there. Don't worry about it now babe.' He brushed it off.

Now Adam had told me that I was holding him back, it was all I could think about. Hanging out with Adam wasn't fun anymore. All he could talk about was going to Utah, and having an adventure – an adventure without me.

I understood that Adam wanted to have some fun, but it was so sudden. Most of all, I couldn't understand how Adam could promise me that he was going to save me from my mom, only to back out six months before I turned eighteen, when he could whisk me away.

• • •

In February, a month and a half before the prom, my mom gave me $50 to get a dress. I was desperate to reconnect with Adam, so I asked him to come shopping with me, to help pick out a dress and a matching tie for him. I wasn't sure if he was leaving before the prom or not. I hoped that picking out a matching outfit would help convince him to stay. I was desperate. It was weird, the more he hurt me, the more I wanted to win him back. It was just like how things were with Mom.

The dress I picked was a beautiful teal colour. The bust was covered in black lace and the bottom of the dress was decorated with black flowers, and the hem had the same lace as the bust. We found a tie for Adam that matched perfectly.

• • •

Several days later, Adam delivered the bad news. He *was* going to Utah, and he was leaving the day of the prom. He had somehow scraped enough money together to share a ride with someone. I hung up, and raced to his house. I felt desperate. When I showed up, I grabbed his hand, and led Adam to his room.

'Adam, I can't let you do this. I don't understand how you think I was going to be okay with you going away for six months. You promised me. You promised me you would save me from my mom and my house,' I sobbed.

He let go of my hand and threw his hands up in the air with irritation.

'Are you breaking up with me? If you are, just come out and say it. I'm not going to let you hold me back.'

'If you're going, then we're done,' I said, choking on my words.

Adam started to cry. He took a deep breath, stood up and ushered me out of the room.

'Then we're done here. Have a nice life,' he mumbled.

I left without saying anything else. I brushed past Will in the kitchen on my way out. Will noticed I was crying and tried to grab my arm, but I yanked it free and left. When I got home, my eyes were red and puffy, and Mom gave me a hug.

'You broke up with him, didn't you?' she guessed.

I didn't want to talk to her, I didn't have any words left I was so distraught.

Adam tried to call me the weekend before my prom. I let it ring through to the answerphone because I didn't want to be reminded of his voice. After a few minutes a voicemail popped up. Apprehensively, I listened to what he had to say.

'Hey babe, uh, I mean Britney. I'm leaving in a couple of days, and I didn't like how our last conversation went. I want to meet up with you to talk. Call me back, I love you ... ah shit, I mean bye.'

I was on my bed, studying for a biology test. I grabbed a pillow to try and stifle my sobs. I was a wreck; I had no idea why he had called. *He still loves me. Does he want to tell me he's not leaving?* I thought, with some hope.

I calmed myself down so I wouldn't sound like a nervous wreck, and then I picked up the phone. I scrolled through to find his number, and then I stared at the screen for a while. I wanted him to tell me he was going to stay. I finally pushed the call button, my heart was beating faster with every ring. Just as I was about to hang up, Adam answered.

'I didn't think you were going to call me back,' he said.

I tried to sound like I didn't care. 'What do you want? I'm busy, that's what took so long,' I shrugged him off.

Adam started pleading for my time. It was a nice feeling to have the tables turned.

'I need to see you. I don't want our last moments with each other to be bitter. I don't want you to hate me. Please, please, see me,' he begged.

The moment was fleeting. I felt crushed again. Adam was still going to Utah, he just wanted us to be on better terms. I started to get choked up. My voice was breaking as I agreed to meet.

'Fine, how is after school on Wednesday? I'll pick you up,' I said.

'Awesome, I'll be ready. I love ...' he started, and then hung up.

Every day that led up to Wednesday was torture. I wanted Adam back, badly. I wanted to talk to him – I missed talking about our days. I wanted someone to vent to when I had had a bad day with Mom or the mess. I wanted someone I felt comfortable with and trusted. I wanted my best friend back.

• • •

Wednesday finally came. I skipped out of school early and I rushed over to Adam's house as fast as I could. I was so anxious to see him. He was waiting for me outside as I pulled into his drive. I stepped out of my car and we awkwardly stood around, not knowing what to say. We headed inside and sat on the couch. Adam finally broke the silence.

'I've missed you so much.'

I didn't care about anything he had to say, except whether he had changed his mind about staying. Angrily, I said, 'So are you leaving or not?'

'I'm leaving. But I'll be back for you,' he smiled.

I started to cry.

'So what does this mean for us? If you're coming back then are we staying together?'

'You wanted to break up with me, so we're going to stay broken up,' he decided. 'I still want to talk to you though. You're my best friend,' he said, reaching for my hand.

I jerked it away. It was all on his terms.

'So you're going to go to Utah, hook up with a bunch of chicks and when you've had your full, come back for me?' I snapped.

He shook his head vigorously, like I'd got it all wrong.

'No. I'm not going to be able to get you out of my mind. I'd feel like I'd be cheating on you. And besides, I don't think I could hook up with anyone.

I'm so comfortable with you – I wouldn't know what to do if I was with someone else.'

'Really?' I asked, grabbing his hand.

'Really.' he whispered, leaning in close.

We kissed passionately. My body was aching for him and his for me. We cuddled for what seemed like hours. I didn't want to leave, but I knew drawing the moment out would make it even harder to say goodbye.

'I'm going to miss you,' I said, kissing him goodbye.

I felt happy as I drove home. *Adam is going to come back, he's not going to mess around with other girls while he's gone, we're just taking a break*. I turned on the radio and belted out whatever song was playing.

• • •

But the bubble burst as soon as I pulled into my drive. He had left me to deal with my mom on my own. For the past three years I'd always had someone to run to for support. Now I was all alone.

I threw myself into my work. I was studying for a test when Mom got home.

'Hey kiddo. How was your day?' she asked.

'It was all right,' I shrugged.

Later that night, the thought of not having Adam to save me started to burn, deep in my stomach. He was supposed to be there for me, tell me everything would be all right, whisk me away the moment I turned eighteen. I couldn't sleep. I just lay there, feeling empty. The tears wouldn't stop. *Adam was the only person that understood me, the only person I was comfortable around.* As I lay in the darkness, I could hear the rain start. The noise wasn't coming from the windows though, like in any normal house. The rain pounded through the hole in the roof and into the buckets in my mom's room. It was a squalid reminder of what I had to face, alone.

CHAPTER 18

As I wobbled on my bed, in front of my mirror, in nothing but a bra and panties, I slid on the dress Adam and I had picked out. I couldn't help but cry. I wiped my eyes and blotted them dry. I sat down on my bed and started working on my hair. I wasn't trying to impress anyone – I didn't really care how I looked.

I pulled my hair into an up-do. There were lumps in my hair and I couldn't be bothered to flatten them out. It wasn't even, but it was good enough. Instead of putting on foundation, blush, eyeshadow, eyeliner, mascara and lipstick, I just put on eyeliner. I put no effort into getting ready. I didn't even shave my legs.

I looked at myself one last time, shrugged and fell back onto my bed. I didn't want to go to my senior prom alone. I was going to meet up with friends, but it wasn't the same.

Mom walked in my room a few minutes later. 'You about ready to go?' she asked sweetly.

'I guess. I just want to get this night over with,' I mumbled.

Mom sat on the edge of my bed.

'You know, Adam didn't define you. You are a beautiful, strong, young lady. Please have a fun night.' They were nice words, but it was too little too late for me.

I was screaming on the inside. *No, he didn't define me, but he was supposed to be my saviour from you. You got in the way of our happiness. You tried everything you could to stop us being happy. You made it so hard for us to see each other.*

I resented Mom for controlling me. I resented her for robbing me of what all my other friends had had – a normal childhood.

I sat up and put on my high heels. I went to the bathroom to brush my teeth, but I tripped and lurched forwards. My heel had got stuck on a trash bag. I freed my foot only to find my heel was now covered in brown goo.

I kicked the wall in frustration, slipped my shoe off and rinsed it in the sink. I looked in the mirror as I was washing away the gunk. I looked ridiculous. My eyes were red and puffy, my hair was a mess – I obviously didn't care. I managed to get the goo off my shoe, brushed my teeth and headed out. When I got to my car, I realised there was now a grocery bag wrapped around my shoe.

'God fucking damn it,' I yelled, pulling it off and tossing it out the door.

I drove to the banquet hall, where my prom was being held. Most of the parking spots were already taken, so I pulled into the back. I sat there for half an hour, smoking one cigarette after another, finding the will to get out and face the world. As I was exhaling, there was a sharp tap on my window. I jumped and I threw the cigarette at my feet to try and snuff it out.

Tara, my lab partner from biology, had a big grin on her face. She opened the door and sat in the passenger seat.

'Drive,' she said, pulling out a big bag of weed.

'You don't have to tell me twice,' I said, starting the car.

'I've been looking for you for the last hour. I figured us "dateless girls" would want a session so we didn't have to think about our guys,' she said, rolling a joint.

'You got that right. You know, Adam helped pick this dress out for me to wear?' I reminisced.

'Oh, hon. I'm sorry, that really sucks. Where are we going?'

'Just to my normal smoke spot,' I said, pulling into a small park.

I pulled over to the spot behind the rubbish bins, and got out.

'Where now?' Tara asked.

'Follow me. There's a tree that fell over, which someone has turned into a bench,' I explained, walking into the woods.

I heard her shut the door, when she said, 'But I'm in heels.'

'It's not far, just walk on your tiptoes,' I waited for her to catch up. I took the joint and hit it, letting the high take over my body.

We smoked three joints, the whole time talking about our exes, and about the biology test we'd taken the day before, then headed back to the prom.

I dropped Tara off at the entrance so she wouldn't mess up her heels. As I was getting out of the car, Nancy ran over and gave me a big hug.

'You look good,' she said, looking me over.

'Thanks. So do you,' I beamed.

We hurried inside, meeting up with the rest of our friends. Every negative thought I'd had that day vanished when I felt the beat of the music. I let it take over me. I danced with my friends, free and happy. After a few hours, I was having a great time, I completely forgot about Adam.

• • •

I went home to change into some clothes for the after-prom parties. A bus was ready to cart everyone from one event to another. We could do bowling, breakfast, coffee, ice cream, the pier and even the YMCA. I met up with Nancy and some of our other friends. I tried to enjoy myself, but once again all I could think of was Adam, and how he wasn't here with me, how he was in a car travelling across the country.

It was 4 a.m. by the time I got home. I quietly made my way up the stairs, trying not to wake up my mom. I was only five steps up, when I laughed at how stupid I was being. Mom knew I was out. Old habits don't die easy – I was making my way up the stairs like I used to do when I'd sneak over to Adam's in the middle of the night.

I straightened my back and walked up the stairs normally, crashing into my bed. I didn't even bother taking my clothes off. Just before I drifted off to sleep, I reached for my memory box. I pulled everything out and I carefully laid it next to me on the bed. There were two poems Adam had written me, the gold and diamond ring he'd got me for my sixteenth birthday, a leaf that had stuck in my hair when we'd had sex in the fort, concert and movie tickets from dates, and the tie he was supposed to wear for prom.

After I'd read the poems dozens of times, I put everything back in the box, except for the ring and tie. I tied the tie around my wrist like a bracelet and slid the ring back on. The tan line was still on my finger even though I hadn't worn the ring for weeks. I fell asleep thinking about how much I was going to miss Adam.

• • •

The weeks that followed prom were terrible. The person I got out of bed for, who I lived for, who I put up with my shitty life for, was no longer in my life. I stopped coordinating my outfits, stopped wearing make-up, stopped brushing my hair – I stopped caring. Every day I'd wear the same thing to school – tracksuit bottoms or pyjama trousers and a big black zip-up hoodie.

My mom asked me the same question, every day, after school. She wanted to know how I was doing. I was working on an essay when she asked me again. I shrugged my shoulders and continued writing. Mom huffed loudly with irritation.

'Stop moping around. It's pathetic. Adam's gone, and he's probably not coming back. It's time to move the fuck on,' she snapped.

Since Adam left, she wouldn't stop yelling at me. She'd tell me I wasn't going out with my friends enough, that I was sleeping too much, that I was crying too much, that I didn't care about myself anymore. She just nagged and nagged. I would have thought she felt sorry for me if she hadn't used the fact I had more free time to her advantage. My chore load after school was doubled, and I had to drive the rubbish to my grandparents' house myself, instead of going with my mom.

• • •

There are two things I remember about my graduation. Firstly, that Adam wasn't there to share it with me, and secondly, that it marked the start of sewage problems in our house.

I got up to use the bathroom one evening and when I lifted the lid I saw a poop in the bowl. I flushed, impatiently waiting for it to go down. I checked again while pulling down my trousers. The poop was still in the bowl. I cried out for Mom.

'Come plunge the toilet. I have to go to the bathroom,' I yelled.

'You do it, you're right there,' she shouted back.

I grabbed the plunger in anger and marched into the living room, where my mom was sitting.

'It's not my shit. Please take care of it, I have to pee super bad,' I said, thrusting the plunger into her hand.

She rolled her eyes, and got up to unblock the toilet.

'There, you can pee now princess,' Mom sneered, walking past me.

From then on, my mom would poop in the middle of the night and not flush it away. I'd wake up in the mornings and the toilet wouldn't flush, not even when we plunged it. My mom left for work one day with the toilet full of her excrement. I flushed and plunged that thing, until I was sure it was going to overflow.

Air bubbles blew up from the brown abyss. The first one caught me off guard, when it surfaced – it sprayed my knees. Gagging, I took a step back, stumbling over a shoe that had lost its mate long ago. Regaining myself, I jumped in the tub and quickly washed my legs off. I wasn't sure if I could smell it on me, or if the smell lingered in the air, but I had to get out of the bathroom.

I couldn't go to the bathroom with shit in the bowl. I was afraid some of it would splash up onto me. I thought my mom was disgusting enough, so the thought her excrement touching me made me retch. So I grabbed my keys, ran downstairs to my car, and raced over to my church. It was only about a mile away and I knew the access code.

pulled up and got out, I didn't even bother turning my car off, I had to go to the bathroom that badly.

I was so desperate, I punched in the wrong security code, twice. The red light flashed, and the device buzzed urgently. I slowed my fingers down, entered the code again, and breathed a sigh of relief when the light flashed green. I ran to the bathroom; I was finally peeing in a clean area.

It didn't matter how much I pleaded with Mom, she refused to get the toilet fixed. She was terrified of people seeing the house after the last workman turned his nose up at the job, so she just let it get worse and worse. I stopped using the toilet at home and rushed to the church every time I needed to go. Strangely, nobody questioned why I was at church several times a day, they were just happy to see me.

That summer was terrible. It was supposed to be the summer of a lifetime – the last summer as a kid before you go off to college. Instead, I was stuck at home, alone, with the trash and the barely working toilet. I wanted to get out more, but Nancy had a full-time job, and more times than not, my mom wouldn't let me use the car, which was still hers, even though she was borrowing my grandparents' spare car. I did as many sports as possible, just so I could use the changing-room showers.

It was halfway through the summer, when we got a call on the house phone. These days the house phone was kept for emergencies only, and not many people had the number. My mom looked confused when she answered it. She looked at me strangely and took the phone to her room.

I tried to listen to what she was saying but I had to give up in the end. After a few minutes, she came back into the living room with a mangled expression on her face.

'That was Will. Firstly, he's really drunk. Secondly, he and Lisa want you to spend the night. They miss you.'

'Tonight?' I asked, surprised.

'Yeah, if you want to go, then go for it,' she said, sitting down.

I jumped at the opportunity to leave the house. I grabbed my pyjamas and left.

• • •

When I pulled up, I was suddenly really nervous. *I know they just invited me over, but do they think any less of me now I'm not with Adam. Are they going to treat me differently?*

I needn't have worried. I got out and met Will who was just back from walking the dogs. He gave me a big hug. 'Hey kid. We missed you.'

'I missed you guys too,' I beamed. I felt like crying.

We hung out the rest of the night, catching up on the past few months. When they went to bed, I lay on the couch, waiting for the house to fall silent. When I was positive that everyone was asleep, I slid into Adam's old room. I inhaled the air – it still smelled like him. I sat on the edge of the bed, reminiscing about the time we spent together.

The room was bare. He didn't leave much behind. As I was skimming past his dresser, I noticed one of the drawers had something sticking out of it. I quietly tugged it open to reveal some of his clothes. I grabbed the shirt on top, slipped it over my head, and inhaled deeply. My head was swimming with memories of him.

I rummaged through the drawer and pulled out a few more shirts. I stuffed them into my bag and then fell onto his bed. I drifted to sleep, comforted that I was finally sleeping in Adam's bed, even if he wasn't in it with me.

I woke up to some commotion going on in the living room. I stumbled out to see Lisa's look of relief.

'Oh thank God. We didn't know where you were. We thought you were on the couch. Where were you?'

My cheeks flushed red with embarrassment.

'I slept in Adam's room. I went in there when you guys had gone to bed. I'm sorry, I just wanted to … I don't know. I'm sorry,' I mumbled.

'Hon, it's okay. I completely understand. You can take that shirt too if you want,' she signalled to a shirt poking out of my bag.

I was even more embarrassed. I sat down next to Will and he kindly changed the subject.

'So what have you been doing this summer? What are your plans for this fall?'

I slumped back into the couch as I was reminded of the house and the blocked toilet, and no Adam.

'I've done nothing this summer. I've babysat, but that's it. I'm just waiting to go to college. I'll have a dorm, my mom won't be there. I can start fresh, no mess.'

It felt good to say those words. I hadn't thought

about what college really meant until that moment. I'd just gone through the motions of applying to do a course in media studies in Springfield. I savoured the taste of those words – no mess. New life.

CHAPTER 19

I didn't want to pack too soon because I couldn't cope with the thought of trudging through the trash to find all my possessions. Three days before I left for college, I finally started packing. I had no clue where to start, clothes were drying on the porch or strewn across the basement. Some of my clean clothes were upstairs, folded in my dresser or stacked at the end of my bed, and others were on the broken dryer downstairs. Overwhelmed, I took a deep breath. *Just grab all of your clothes and pile them on your bed.*

I had two suitcases full to the brim with clothes by the time I was done. Next, I organised my wash bag with all of my new shampoos, soaps and make-up. I set my bags next to my bedroom door in a tidy row. It was a sign of things to come – my new life would be tidy and clean.

• • •

After an hour's drive, Mom pulled into the university grounds. I was shocked at how much energy and life the place had. Parents were dropping kids off, moms were crying and dads were beaming with pride. The football team chipped in, carrying freshmen's heavy stuff to the rooms. We parked in front of my dorm, and my heart started to race.

Finally, I was getting out of my mom's house. It was actually going to happen. I was nervous about meeting my roommate though. I didn't know who I'd be paired with. We had filled in a questionnaire – the questions like 'Are you a morning person?' or 'What is your major?' were easy to answer. I got stuck when I came across 'Are you a messy or tidy person?' I didn't really know how to answer that. I kept my room as clean as I could without a vacuum or a duster, and I tried keeping the area around my stool clean, but I could also tolerate mess. I'd put up with squalor for eighteen years. After much confusion and anxiety, I finally ticked that I was a clean person, and hoped it was true.

We opened the trunk to unload, and my cheeks burned with embarrassment. Even though she had only been using it for a few months, the car was already trashed. I was struggling, trying to tug the mini-fridge from out of the trunk, when two of the football players came over to help.

'Don't worry about it. I'm all set,' I said, embarrassed at the thought of them seeing the mess.

They laughed at my feeble attempt to do it by myself, but they were polite enough not to say anything about the trash.

'We're here to be muscle. Which room is yours?' one of them asked as he carried the fridge along the path.

'4126. Thanks,' I said, grabbing my suitcase, and chasing after them.

I dodged others moving in, and followed the guys who had my fridge upstairs to my room. The door was open and my roommate had already chosen the left side of the room. I didn't care, I was just glad I was starting a new life.

'We're going to put this here for now. If you need help moving it later, just grab one of us. Bye ladies,' the footballer winked at me, and then left.

My mom had already introduced herself to my roommate and her parents.

'Hi, I'm Britney,' I held out my hand from behind my mom.

'I'm Kim. I can't wait for us to get to know each other,' she said giving me a hug.

We both unloaded the rest of our things. Kim's parents gave her a quick hug goodbye. Mom, on the other hand, lingered. She sat on my bed and grabbed the photo album I had brought with me. As she flipped through the photos of my graduation, adventures I'd had with Adam, library events I shared with Nancy – she started to cry.

'I can't believe my baby is all grown up,' she sniffed, looking at me, with tears falling down her face.

'Yep, all grown up. Don't you have to be at work early tomorrow?' I asked, annoyed at her public display of emotion. I knew it was mean of me, but I'd had enough of her mood swings. I didn't want her tainting my chance of a new life.

She continued to flip through the album, until, 'I guess I'll leave.' She wiped her eyes.

She got up, and gave me a big hug, sobbing into the small of my neck. I squeezed her back quickly and dropped my arms to my sides. She still held onto me, tightly. I cleared my throat loudly, hoping she would take the hint to let go of me. She pulled back, and held both of my shoulders. Her eyes were puffy and still moist. Her fringe stuck to her wet cheeks.

'I love you,' she said, walking out of the door.

Kim was pretending to fold her clothes.

'That was painfully awkward,' she cringed.

I giggled and apologised. 'Yeah, I just wanted her gone,' I said, studying my new room. It was a blank canvas that I could transform into something that was 'me'. I was finally free.

I suddenly felt very emotional. The familiar feeling of tears prickled my eyes. I couldn't let my new roommate see me cry though, so I pinched my arm to hold them back. If only Kim knew what this room meant to me. I wished I could share what I was feeling, but I didn't want her to think I was a freak.

Kim flipped on the TV she had brought with her. My face lit up, it was the first TV I'd ever had in my own room. I started unpacking my clothes, while watching the screen. So much was new to me. I was experiencing the first time I could fold my clean clothes away into a cupboard, and then Kim surprised me with my first Hoover.

After a couple of hours of getting our room in order, Kim pulled the vacuum out. I stopped her. It was too big a deal for me to miss.

'Can I do it? I've never had a Hoover before,' I squealed with delight.

She gave me a look to say I was weird, but then handed it to me.

'Seriously?' she giggled.

I flipped on the vacuum, excited by the loud sound.

'Yeah, my mom isn't a clean person. I'm glad I'm starting fresh,' I shouted over the noise.

After I had finished vacuuming, Kim and I walked to the freshmen rooms. It had a coffee shop, convenience store and a food court. I grabbed a burrito and she bought a sandwich. We scanned the cafe for an open table. The hall was so packed, we had to share with other freshmen.

'So, I want to make a cleaning schedule. Is that cool?' I blurted out.

'Yeah, but we need to talk to the others who we share our bathroom with,' she said, between bites.

'Cool. Well for our room, you vacuum once every two weeks, and I'll do it the other weeks. Let's make sure we keep our clothes in one spot, clean up the sink after we use it, and, apart from that, we're all set,' I said in one breath, because I wasn't sure how she was going to react.

She swallowed hard on her drink.

'Yeah, I'll do my part if you do yours,' she said.

'Fair enough,' I smiled. I felt incredibly relieved we'd worked something out. The anxiety of making a new life, without mess, had been eating me up.

We finished lunch, and headed back to the dorms. We knocked on our neighbour's door. The one who answered was already drunk. As she waved us in, she tripped over their rug and landed hard on her knees. Giggling, she looked up and said, 'I'm Mary.'

Her roommate rolled her eyes, and helped her to her feet.

'Hi, I'm Jessica,' she said dragging Mary to her bed.

'It looks like someone is starting early. It's barely dark,' Kim laughed.

'Yeah, she's my cousin. I didn't want to room with her, but her mom knew she needed a babysitter,' she sounded annoyed.

I stepped forward to move things along.

Our room was an exact mirror of theirs, with the bathroom in the middle. The bathroom had a toilet and a shower with a curtain. The doors to the bathroom could be locked from each room. We just needed to make sure we knocked before going in.

'I'm Britney, and this is Kim. We're your neighbours. We wanted to say "Hi" – and make a cleaning schedule,' I said in a rush, shaking Jessica's hand.

Mary laughed hysterically from her bed. Jessica ushered us into the hallway.

'I'm sorry, don't mind her. Can we talk in your room? I don't want to deal with her,' she whispered.

We walked to our door, and let ourselves inside. Jessica sat next to me, on my bed, while Kim sat on hers.

'So luckily, we're all on the meal plan so we don't need to worry about the kitchen. I thought we should clean the bathroom once a week. Individually, we only have to clean it once a month. I'll do it first,' I said, anxious to get things sorted.

'I'll do second,' Jessica volunteered, cheerfully.

'Kim you want to take third and I'll tell Mary she gets the last week?'

Nodding her head, Kim said, 'It sounds good to me.'

We began to chat more about ourselves, and had only been talking for around five minutes, when we heard a loud crash coming from the bathroom. Jessica shook her head, and murmured something under her breath. She opened the door to the bathroom to find Mary passed out on the floor, with the rod and curtain strewn beside her.

We weren't sure if she had passed out because of the alcohol, or because she hit her head. Jessica dragged Mary by her feet to their room, but was struggling. I grabbed Mary's arms and helped Jessica heave her into bed. It made a change to see someone else dealing with a family member.

There were no classes during the first week of college. It was a time for the new students to get their rooms organised, and for us to make friends. I'd never felt so relaxed – I didn't have to worry about my mom breathing down my neck. I didn't have to clean up a mess that wasn't mine. I wasn't waist deep in rubbish. I felt cleaner, prettier and healthier than I ever had.

I was so glad Kim and I had hit it off. We had so much in common – we liked the same music, TV shows and clothes. We became friends instantly. That first week we decided to go to a party we had heard about. It was in the apartments off the campus, so we jumped in Kim's truck and headed over. We got there for around midnight, and as soon as we turned into the street, we knew which house it was. There were dozens of people hanging out on the lawn, and the windows kept lighting up from the flashing strobe light inside.

Kim parked on the street and we could hear the bass of the music, booming. Kim didn't drink or smoke, but she didn't mind that I smoked as long as I didn't bring any weed into our room. I was fine with that. When we walked inside, we were immediately handed cups full with beer. Kim discarded hers on the side of the steps. Not trusting what was in it,

I did the same. People were drunk and stumbling all over the place. It was way too loud to talk to anyone. We left after a few minutes.

'I'm sorry, but that's just too crazy for me,' Kim said, starting her car.

Buckling up, I said, 'Don't feel bad, me too. I party with friends, not random strangers who I can't trust.'

'Want to get ice cream and watch *The Notebook*. I know some people from my high school I can invite. Do you know anyone?' she smiled.

I scrolled through my phone, and found a couple of friends from high school who also attended my college that I could call. We swung by the store to grab a big tub of ice cream. When we got back to our dorm, a few people were already waiting outside for us. Only one of my friends was there. She had a big bag with her, and greeted me with a massive hug.

'We're going to have a real girly night. I've got a ton of nail polishes, and toppings to go on the ice cream,' she boasted.

Five of us went upstairs to our dorm, and got the girls' night started. We painted our nails while watching the film, and ate ice cream and cried during the sad parts. For the first time in a while, I was having fun. I didn't think about Adam, I was no longer stressed about living with my mom or in the house. I was hanging out with friends, in my own room, away from everything bad. At the end of the movie everyone was tired because of how late it was. Instead of going back to their dorms, they slept in our room. Fourteen years late, I was finally getting my sleepover!

I woke up in the middle of the night needing to go to the bathroom. I started to frantically search for my flip-flops. The adrenaline shook me wide awake and I realised where I was. I wasn't at home, but in my dorm room. I didn't need my flip-flops to go to the bathroom. I could walk around barefoot and not worry about stepping in puddles of piss. I tiptoed over the girls sleeping on the floor, glad I didn't have to worry about stepping in any nasty stuff. It was going to take me a while to get used to this.

• • •

We decided to meet up for the football game the next day. It would be Adam's birthday, so I was glad I was going to be busy with friends and watching the game, instead of thinking about him. Our conversations on the phone had got better, but it was still hard knowing that Adam wasn't going to be home for another two months.

The game was packed, so we couldn't find seats in the student section. We ended up getting spots on the fence, right by the side line. During halftime, everyone had to use the bathroom, except for me. I was just thinking how bored I was when I got a call from Adam.

'Hey babe, I've got a surprise for you,' he said, excitedly.

'Really, what is it? Are you coming here for a visit?' I asked, jokingly.

'Even better. I'm in Illinois, on my way back,' he chirped.

I dropped my phone, I was so stunned. I regained my composure and scrambled around in the dirt for my cell.

'I'm sorry. How long until I see you?' I stuttered.

'I'm still working on that. We've been driving for twenty hours already. We'll be there in about two hours. I'm going to try to get you soon,' he said, optimistically.

'Please, please, come get me,' I pleaded.

'I don't think I'll be able to until tomorrow. There is no room in the back because the car is packed with all of our stuff. I can barely fit in the back seat. Jerry is exhausted and doesn't want to unload the car and drive an hour to get you, and another hour to get back,' he explained with disappointment. Jerry was Adam's best friend, the guy who convinced Adam to go out to Utah in the first place.

I racked my brain for ideas.

'I can drive the rest of the night as long as Jerry gets here. Just come get me,' I negotiated.

'I'll run it by him. Gotta go. Love you,' he said, hanging up suddenly.

The halftime show was coming to an end and I was having a meltdown. *Adam is here in Illinois, I might be seeing him in just a few hours.* He wasn't supposed to be back for another two months. I had to get ready – I needed to shower, to shave my legs, do my make-up and find some nice clothes to wear.

My hands were shaking as I started to text Kim the news that I needed to leave the game. I was halfway through typing the message, when one of her friends came back from the bathroom.

'Hey, I've got to go. Can you watch our spot?' I said, nervously.

'Yeah, is everything okay?' she asked, concerned.

'Everything's fine. My boyfriend is back in town, he's been gone for four months,' I squealed excitedly, and then I took off.

As I was running back to the dorms, Adam called. I was out of breath as I answered.

'We're coming to get you in an hour. You have to drive the rest of the night,' he said.

'Okay, I'll be ready. Call me when you get here,' I said, shouting with joy.

• • •

I ran up the stairs to my floor, and I dropped my keys as I had so much adrenaline rushing through me. Finally inside, I packed my bag before taking a shower. I'd never spent the whole night with Adam at his house before.

I looked through my wardrobe. My eyes grew wide as saucers looking in my underwear drawer. *Bring them all. A girl can never have enough panties.* Emptying the drawer, I moved onto trousers. *I guess my three cutest ones will work. Now for shirts, my wardrobe has matured since I last saw him, but I've kept the old stuff to lounge in. Will he like my new look with blouses and sweaters, or my old T-shirt look? Get a mix of both – three each will be enough.*

I was overthinking what I should bring, and eventually packed my bag like I would do to spend the night anywhere else. I jumped in the shower, wanting to wash my hair too, but there wasn't enough time. I rinsed off and jumped out. Dressed in just my towel, I frantically tore through my side of the room. I turned, and looked back at the mess in the bathroom. I couldn't leave it like that. Even if it meant I was going to be late, I had to clean it up. *I'm never going to be like my mom.*

I felt a sense of relief. For the first time my clothes were really clean. I didn't have to sniff them to see if the odour of the house clung to them. All of my clothes now had a place. My underwear and pyjamas went in the top drawer, shirts went in the second drawer, and pants went in the third drawer. Dresses and blazers were in the wardrobe along with my shoes.

I was putting the finishing touches on my make-up, when my phone rang. I jumped, and drew an awful black line across my cheek.

'Hello?' I asked, wiping the eyeliner off my face.

'We're just down the road. Start heading to the parking lot,' Adam said, hanging up.

That'll do, I thought, looking in the mirror. Just as I was about to move away, I actually looked at myself. I was much happier. I didn't have to always be on edge anymore about my mom's mood swings, and because my surroundings were better, I felt I looked better too.

I gazed at my tidy room, smiling. Then I grabbed my bag, phone and laptop, and headed for the parking lot. My heart was racing – I was so excited to see Adam again. I was trying to picture what he looked like, and I hoped he would still like me.

I put my bag on the sidewalk, and sat on the low brick wall next to the road that cut through the campus. I glared at every car that passed, trying to make out if it was Jerry or Adam. My phone rang.

'I can see you. Look to your left, I'm waving and walking towards you,' Adam surprised me.

I scanned the car park in front of me, and I finally spotted Adam coming towards me. I shoved my phone in my pocket, and sprinted across the road, narrowly missing a car. I didn't care about the traffic; I was going to finally hold him. Adam's arms were stretched out, waiting for me. I jumped into him, wrapping my arms around his neck and my legs around his waist. I started sobbing because I was so happy that I could finally hold him.

I was still clutching Adam as I unwrapped my legs and stood up. I pulled his face to mine and kissed him hard. I wiped my eyes – I probably looked like a mess, but I didn't care. I finally had Adam back.

'You left your bag over there,' Adam sniffed, he was also crying.

He grabbed my hand as we walked over to fetch my bag.

'Let me get it, babe,' he said, picking it up.

I grabbed onto his arm instead, I didn't want to let him go. We walked up to Jerry's car, and found him lying across the back seat with exhaustion.

'We have to go to Taco Bell back home. We're meeting some people. Britney, please tell me you're still driving?' he said, without opening his eyes.

'Not a problem.' I said, jumping in the driver's seat.

Adam took the passenger seat next to me. It was an hour's drive to the Taco Bell. The ride was silent except for Jerry's light snores coming from the back. I held onto Adam's hand tightly for the entire journey. I didn't want to stop touching him, not for even a second.

• • •

The three of us finally arrived at Adam's parent's house at 3 a.m. Everyone was sleeping, so Jerry crashed on the couch, while Adam and I went to his bedroom. Even though he was exhausted, we stayed up for the entire night, cuddling and talking about the time we spent apart.

I was glad he was back early, but felt bad as to why. He told me the last month they were working, Adam and his co-workers weren't getting paid what they deserved. Their boss made it clear that things weren't going to change, so instead of working for free, he and Jerry came back.

Despite all that, Adam seemed much happier than when he'd left. He talked about the mountains of Utah and how he fell in love with his surroundings. Instead of playing video games, he would go for a hike through the trails. And he had plans. Even though he didn't get fully paid for what he worked, he had a few hundred dollars and was going to work construction with his dad.

I told him about my new life at college. Adam understood my excitement because he was the only one who knew how awful my old life had been. But even he was shocked when I told him that I had used my first vacuum cleaner a week ago.

On Monday morning, Adam dropped me off a few hours before my classes started. All the problems or issues we'd had in the past somehow didn't matter anymore. We both understood that we were starting over.

• • •

I was dreading Christmas break. Mom was expecting me to go home for the whole month. I hadn't been back to that house since she first dropped me off at college, and I had no idea what the state of the house was. I imagined there would be piles more rubbish now I hadn't been there to clear up. On a car ride back to Adam's in November he asked me what I was going to do.

'So what are our plans for Christmas?' he asked tentatively.

'Nothing, I think. My mom is picking me up and I'm staying with her until classes resume after the New Year,' I said, shuddering.

'Maybe it's time to leave? You're an adult, and you don't need to live in filth,' Adam said.

It was a good point. I just wasn't sure I was brave enough yet.

CHAPTER 20

My mom picked me up for Christmas break, after my last class on Tuesday afternoon. My stomach was churning as we pulled up to the house. I was praying that the place would be cleaner. I hadn't talked about the state of the house once to her since I'd left; I'd hoped that she would have got her act together. When I opened the door, I wasn't shocked to see that the laundry room hadn't changed. Clothes were haphazardly tossed on the dryer. I couldn't tell which clothes on the ground were dirty or clean. The dryer still hadn't been fixed, so clothes were hung from nails on the wall, doorknobs and strewn across tables. I headed upstairs, and took a deep breath as I opened the door.

The living room had changed – but not for the better. There was more trash than ever, and more laundry strung up all over the place. The smell hit me like a bulldozer. The house smelt like mould and mildew mixed with the odour of something rotting. The further I walked into the pit, the more pronounced the smell of Mom's piss became. Just walking past my mom's room made my eyes water, it was so bad.

I dropped my bag on my bed, shaking my head in disgust as I kicked the trash out of my room, and back into the hallway. In the short time I had been gone, rubbish had started spilling into my bedroom. When I returned to the living room. My precious stool was completely covered in trash. I grabbed a trash bag, and started throwing everything away. Takeaway containers, grocery bags, newspapers, used sanitary pads, tissues, they all went into the trash bag. I lifted a newspaper to reveal a pile of clothes stacked high on the stool, covered in stains where the takeaway containers had leaked.

I tossed the clothes down the stairs angrily.

'What are you doing? Those clothes were clean,' she barked.

'No, they were the ones on the stool. They were under all of the trash,' I reasoned.

Nodding her head, she said, 'Yeah, I know. Those were clean.'

I looked at her like she was crazy. I went downstairs and grabbed her 'clean' clothes, and threw them on the end of the couch, which was already crowded with even more clothes and rubbish.

I had to go to the bathroom but I dreaded what the state of the toilet would be. I could barely walk down the hallway to the bathroom. There were so many clothes on the ground, covering up rubbish and soda bottles. I had to calculate my steps carefully. I'd twisted my ankle before, stepping on a soda bottle I didn't know was there.

The floor in the bathroom had a rusty colour from my mom's dried period blood. Her blood was also streaked across the filthy bath. I opened the lid of the toilet to reveal an old poop, and red stained toilet paper. I gagged. I dropped the lid and ran out.

I needed to escape. I was desperate for the toilet. I approached my mom who was in front of her computer as usual.

'Did you insure me again on your old car? Am I good to drive? Can I go out?' I asked, urgently.

'Yeah, just be quiet when you come in. I've got to go to work in a few hours,' she said, exhausted. 'Just be in before I have to be at work. I have to be there for 4 a.m., so let's say 3 a.m. People are taking time off because of Christmas, so I'm picking up the extra shifts.'

'3 a.m.? Don't you want to know who I'm hanging out with?' I asked, confused by the freedom she was giving me.

She got up and walked to her bedroom.

'You're eighteen now. You've been living on your own for four months. You're back in town, go hang out with friends.'

This is amazing, I thought. I only wanted to take the car to church so I could go to the bathroom, instead she gave me a free pass until 3 a.m.

I grabbed my purse and my keys, and took off for Adam's house. I wasn't really expecting to see him much over the holiday because I had to babysit during the day on the lead up to Christmas, and Mom of course didn't want me seeing him anymore. But because she didn't ask, I headed over – making a pit stop at church on the way.

Adam and I hung out until 2.30 a.m. Mom was in the shower when I got home, which was a good thing. I smelt of cigarettes and weed, and I didn't want to have to come up with an excuse. Getting high was be the only way to make the thought of staying at home bearable.

Even though I was really baked, I couldn't fall asleep. The smell of the house was nauseating, and I could hear mice crawling around in the box below my mattress. I was afraid to fall asleep. *What if they crawl on me while I'm sleeping? Or worse, bite me?*

Mom finished her shower but I was still awake. She popped her head into my room to make sure I was home. I pretended to be asleep so she wouldn't talk to me. She lingered in the doorway for a while. I just lay there, listening to the mice below my head, scratching and running around.

She finally started getting ready for work, and then left. When I heard her shut the downstairs door, I sat up in my bed. I looked out of the window and waited for her tail lights to disappear into the night. It was snowy and cold outside, but I still opened my bedroom window to smoke a joint Adam had given me. I smoked half of it and felt better, snuffed it out and went to get something to eat.

I was just about to walk into the kitchen when I realised I wasn't wearing my flip-flops. I grabbed my shoes from my bedroom and went to the fridge. There was no food. There wasn't meat to cook, potatoes to boil or takeaway dinners to reheat. There was nothing.

There was no way I was going to sleep in my bed with the mice, so I started searching for somewhere else I could rest my head. My mom's bed was a definite no. I checked the couch, but the upholstery was ripped open and fraying, and the seat was again covered with period blood. I shuddered.

I grabbed my blanket, keys and phone, and went outside to Mom's old car. It was in the driveway, and had a small layer of snow on it. I clambered in, tossing my blanket and phone on the passenger seat. I turned on the engine and blasted out the hot air. When the snow finally melted, I opened the garage door and parked inside.

I crawled over to the passenger seat and pushed the back down, all the way. I huddled under my blanket and set the alarm on my phone for 9 a.m. I had to babysit at 10 a.m., which was in five hours' time. Exhausted, I finally fell asleep, shivering.

• • •

It was nice babysitting, because I had something to do, other than be at home. But that job would stop a couple of days before Christmas Eve and I would be stuck in the house again. It was bitterly cold. Snow was coming in through the hole in the roof, dusting the trash in my mom's room with a white layer.

Mom was on the toilet one morning, peeing, when she called me over to talk to her. I awkwardly looked away from her.

'Can't we do this some other time? You're on the toilet,' I tried to reason.

She shook her head 'No' and carried on.

'It's just real quick. Do you want to go to Florida for spring break? I saw these great deals and if w—'

I interrupted her. I'd had enough.

'The roof needs to be fixed. Use the money you were going to spend on a holiday to get a new roof.'

Laughing it off, she said, 'Oh it's not that bad.'

'Not that bad? It's snowing in your room, right now, as we speak. I got bronchitis six times living in this house. We live like animals, in filth. Why don't you just get a new house?' I shouted.

She looked at me oddly, and defended herself.

'It's fine here. It's messy, but it gets the job done. As for the hole – so what? It's not going to affect me,' she shrugged.

I grabbed my purse, and turned on my heels.

'I'm going to Nancy's. I don't have to babysit until the afternoon. I won't be back too late.'

I took off, not waiting for any objection. I headed to Adam's house. I told him everything my mom had just said. He shook his head in disgust and I saw the anger in his eyes.

'It seems like she doesn't care about you, or herself or anything. She'd rather go on holiday than live properly.'

Burying my face in my hands, I said, 'I can't do this anymore. I have to stay with her another three weeks before I get to go back to college. I'm done. I just don't know what to do.'

Adam grabbed my hand.

'Don't go back. Just stay here and never talk to her again.' he suggested. 'You can still go to college, don't your loans and grants take care of the cost?'

'I can't do that. What about the car? She's going to want it back. And I have to babysit tomorrow until midnight.'

'Okay, so babysit tomorrow, your mom will be sleeping when you get home. I'll come get you,' he said, stroking my cheek.

My head was swimming. I'd never been on my own – I'd always had my mom to fall back on. Adam's words made a mark though. For the first time in my life, I realised I had a choice.

I am an adult now – my mom can't hold onto me anymore, she can't control me.

College is paid for by my grants and loans, she has no say in that matter.

I don't have to live in filth.

I now have a choice and I choose freedom.

'I'm going to do it. I'm sick of the filth, and her, not giving a shit.' I fought away my fears.

'Really?' Adam was shocked. 'I didn't think you would. You've never told her how you really feel.'

'I'm going to do it. I'm sick of all of it. Just be waiting tomorrow evening at the gas station down the street and I'll call you when I'm ready to get picked up. I'll call you as I'm on my way home, just get down there, and then I'll call you again,' I said. I was trembling inside.

• • •

I tucked the kids into bed, cleaned up the mess we had made and watched TV as I waited for their parents to get home from shopping. The entire time with Adam, I was sure I was going to leave my mom. But when it was just me with my thoughts, I started having doubts. *What if she talks me out of it? What is her reaction going to be? Am I even brave enough to talk to her?* I thought it over, and over, until their parents arrived.

I was so nervous on the way home. I kept stopping just to catch my breath. I had no idea what I was going to tell her. When I pulled up, the house was dark. I called Adam while I was in the driveway to let him know he had to go to the gas station to wait for me. My heart was racing. I crept inside and I found Mom sleeping in her room. I shook her leg, trying to wake her up.

'Leave me alone,' she mumbled, while sleeping.

'Mom I want to talk. I'm leaving. For good,' I took a deep breath. She let out a loud snore.

Saying just those words made me sweat and shake. *That'll be enough*, I thought. I wasn't brave enough to say it if she was awake.

I'd only been home a few days, so luckily I hadn't fully unpacked my bag from college. I stuffed the few things I had used back into the bag and went downstairs to call Adam again. As I was dialling his number, my heart ached. *What am I doing?* I thought.

I couldn't just get up and leave in the middle of the night. I quietly made my way back upstairs, and wrote her a note.

Mom,
I can't live like this anymore. The other day you laughed off the fact that you are living in a pigsty. Like I said, we live like animals, and I've seen the other side now. I'm done living in heaps of trash. You need help and a new house. Please

don't worry about me, I'm going to go back to college, and I'm in a safe place.

I love you.

Britney

I put the note on the bathroom counter so she was sure to see it. This time I didn't even care if she heard me leaving. Bravely, I went down the stairs, calling Adam on my way outside. Just in case my mom had heard me leave, I walked across the street to the liquor store, and waited against the side of the building for Adam to get me.

It felt like an eternity, even though it was only a minute. Adam finally pulled into the store parking lot and, as I was getting in, I couldn't help but feel free. I didn't feel bad about leaving in the middle of the night.

I felt like a new person.

I buckled up and Adam looked at me.

'You really did it! I'm proud of you. Do you want to talk?'

Lighting a cigarette, I said, 'Just drive.'

CHAPTER 21

I woke up to my phone going off. Panicking, I didn't know where I was. I rubbed my eyes a few times, and looked across to see Adam lying next to me. Realising where I was, my breathing slowed. *I'm not in my mom's house anymore. I'm safe, next to Adam.*

I grabbed my phone, and there was a text from my mom.

Please come home. I didn't know it was that bad. I didn't know I upset you. I love you.

My heart raced again. *Did I do the wrong thing?* I shook my head to cement my decision. I turned off my phone, and tossed it next to the bed.

'What was that?' Adam mumbled.

'My mom texted me,' I said, snuggling next to him.

'What did she say?' he asked, wrapping his arms around me.

'Nothing,' I replied.

'Well, go back to sleep then,' he said, kissing my cheek.

Listening to Adam snore, I lay awake thinking. It would be my first Christmas without my mom. I was excited that I would have a full-sized Christmas tree for the first time instead of a puny, one-foot-tall tree, balancing on the piles of trash next to the TV. I wouldn't have to pluck my presents out from the rubbish. At the same time, I was worried about Mom. I left in the middle of the night, she didn't even know if I was okay. I didn't know if she was okay without me.

I felt bad that I wasn't going to be able to give much to Lisa or Will. They had been so welcoming, and I knew they were going to get me presents. I know Will liked assorted chocolates, and Lisa wouldn't want me spending money on her anyway. I got them a big box of chocolates, hoping they would like it.

• • •

Christmas with Adam's family was lovely. Relaxing, loving and, more than anything, normal. Just like the Christmases I grew up watching on TV. Right before the New Year, I got a text from Mom:

Return the mobile and your house key and
I won't press charges. If they are not returned
by the first of the year, I will call the police and
have the phone taken back accordingly.

I showed Adam the text. *Is she serious?*

It almost seemed like a trap, making me *have* to go
back to the house. I was almost sure she concocted
an elaborate plan to talk to me face to face.

'She should be at work. Do you want to go return
them now?' I asked him.

'Yeah sure. Let's go,' he said, throwing on a coat.

When we pulled up, I made sure her car wasn't
in the garage. That wasn't enough reassurance, so I
knocked on the door. When she didn't answer, I let
myself in.

'Hello?' I called out. I let out a deep breath of
relief and headed upstairs. It looked like she had
been on a rampage. Dirty dishes in the kitchen were
festering with maggots and mould. It looked like
something had boiled over on the stove, which she
had just left. I had worked on making some space
in the living room before I went, now there wasn't
even a path through the garbage. It was just a heap
of stuff: dirty work clothes, takeaway boxes from
work. The few things that usually had their places

373

were thrown across the room. Piles of stuff were knocked over. It was even worse than when I had left.

I went to my room, and grabbed a few things I hadn't thought of when I had walked out in the night. I went into the bathroom to discover the note I had left, still sitting in the exact same place. My stomach started churning. I felt bad at what I put her through, two days before Christmas. I ran the water out of the tap, and splashed some on my face. Looking into the toothpaste splattered mirror, I shook myself out of it. *You could be living like this*, I thought to myself, grimacing at my surroundings.

I filled the backpack I had brought with me with mementos, and a few extra items of clothing. Before leaving for good, I placed my phone and keys on the stairs. I took a deep breath before shutting the door.

'Goodbye,' I whispered.

CHAPTER 22

Adam dropped me off at college at the end of the Christmas break. Sometimes my mom would try to message me on Facebook, but I eventually blocked her. My grandma or aunt would sometimes message me too, but I didn't responded to them either. I was afraid they would convince me to move back in with my mom. I had no idea what lines Mom was feeding them, and I didn't want to be trapped again. I had just been set free.

After a few months of no contact with my family, I got a message from my Aunt Maxine:

I'm outside your dorm. It's just me, I promise.
Let me take you out to lunch and I've got
Christmas presents for you.

Curious, I looked out my dorm window. Sure enough, my aunt was sitting outside. It looked like she was alone. I threw on a coat, and went outside. As I approached the car, I heard the doors unlock to let me in.

'I just want to give you presents, eat and hear your side,' she said, sweetly.

Nodding my head, we went to a local Mexican restaurant for burritos. As we were waiting for our order to come out, my aunt asked, 'So why did you leave? What happened?'

'I don't know how much you guys know, but Mom hoarded trash. It was out of control,' I said. I was sick at the thought of how I used to live.

She nodded her head sympathetically. 'I know. I helped your mom and your grandma and grandpa clear out the house.'

What? I couldn't believe what I just heard.

'She cleaned it?' I was shocked.

'She's selling it. She bought a new house. Every weekend Grandpa comes over with a big trailer and we all fill it up. We've taken eight trailers of trash out, and the house still isn't empty,' she said.

'It's a lot easier to start over, than to try and fix it all,' I mumbled in disbelief.

Maxine was about to say something else, when she paused. The waitress came over with our burritos, and filled our drinks. Looking to make sure the coast was clear, she whispered, 'I didn't know it was that bad. What happened? How did it get like that?'

I took a bite of the burrito. Where did I begin?

'I don't know. It's been like that ever since I can remember.'

'I'm sorry,' she said.

We didn't talk about the house or Mom after that. It had been a few months since I'd talked with anyone in the family. Going back to my dorm, Maxine followed me up to my room and sat on my bed as I opened presents from her and my grandparents.

That was the last time I spoke with my family. It wasn't a decision I made, it just happened. My mom kept trying to get a hold of me through post and email. I felt bad for never responding, but I didn't know what to say. I was afraid that she would convince me to go back home. I think I must have been angry with them all for letting me live like that for eighteen years. I liked being in my clean room at college, and staying with Adam on the weekends. I was going to move in with him in the summer. Instead of facing her, I ran away, ignoring everything she said to me.

• • •

About a month after Maxine's visit, Adam came to pick me up. Like a gentleman, he grabbed my bag, and put it in the trunk. As we took off, Adam turned to me with a sparkle in his eye.

'I've got a surprise for you.'

'What is it?' I grinned.

'You'll see it when we get there,' he said, playfully.

'Oh, it's at home?' I said, smiling.

Squeezing my hand tight, he said, 'You'll see.'

I was talking about how my week had been when I realised that we weren't taking our usual route home. I was just happy that I was with Adam again, so I shrugged it off, and continued chatting.

We were cruising along the freeway when I saw the exit to get to my mom's house ahead. Seeing the sign made me wonder how she was doing, and where she was in her life. I assumed we were going to pass the exit, but we followed the curve of the road, which led towards my mom's house.

'Where are we going?' I asked urgently.

'I saw something the other day, and I thought you might like it,' he said, smiling.

Memories came flooding back as we drove down the road. It had been almost six months since I had seen the house. The forest near my old home had grown thick. As we passed the trees, I was expecting to see the roof of the house rising above the branches. *What's this? I can't see the roof.*

I sat up, wondering if the trees had grown so much in such a small space of time.

My jaw dropped as we passed the forest. My old house had disappeared. We slowed down so I could get a better look. The house, and all of the trees, were gone. The 'pit' had been filled in. You couldn't even tell there used to be anything there.

'How do you like your surprise?' Adam asked.

'It's beautiful,' I whispered. I was still dazed by the clearing.

Seeing that the house no longer existed felt like my horrible past was erased. I grabbed Adam's hand and squeezed it tightly, smiling the whole time. It was over, it was finally over. I never had to worry about going back, stepping in piss, climbing over trash, driving a mile to use the toilet.

I was so relieved I never had to go back. Adam pressed on the accelerator, and we drove off, into our future together.

EPILOGUE

I finished my freshman year in Springfield but needed to work, so I didn't return for the next college year. But then Adam and I caught the adventure bug and almost overnight we took off. His parents came too, they were also feeling adventurous. Mom had no clue what I was up to.

About a year after I left, Adam and I got pregnant. I was afraid of what Mom would think. Surely she would be mad at me for leaving college. I clearly didn't want her to be part of my life, so why would she want to be involved? Instead of telling her, I just got on with my life.

Coming home from the hospital, I put baby Andrew in the bassinet, tucking the blanket around him. I leaned in, kissing his forehead and whispered, 'Andrew, I promise that you will have a great childhood. You'll have room to run around, any of your friends can spend the night, and I'll do my best to make sure nothing bad happens to you. I love you.'

•••

But Mom hadn't forgotten me. Curious as to if I was still alive, she googled my name and my baby registry came up in the search results. She found out she was a grandma by accident. Less than a month after my son was born she flew out west, where Adam and I have settled.

Instead of being mad at me, she rightfully understood. She was so apologetic about my upbringing. She said that life had just got so overwhelming that she put blinders over her eyes, so she didn't have to deal with the mess or anything else.

She told me she is getting better. She has bought a nice little house downtown, and my grandparents have a key and check up on her a few times a week. Grandma encourages Mom to keep clean, and has made a cleaning schedule so the house doesn't become too overwhelming.

I'm a clean person, but I notice that I will sometimes let a mess slide for a day or so, especially now that I've got Andrew. Even with Adam, the cleaning can be somewhat daunting. So I can understand how being a single working mother would have made things difficult for my mom. But I also know I will do anything for my son, including raising him in a clean and healthy environment. Since leaving home, I've never had bronchitis.

It's still a work in progress, Mom and me, but I'm glad to say she's back in my life.